LIFE WITHOUT FUEL

DISCOVERING ENDLESS ENERGY WITHIN

KRUNAL SHAH

To my parents, whose unwavering support and timeless wisdom have been the foundation of my character and success. Your teachings on integrity, resilience, and love have been the true fuel for my journey.

To my mentors, especially Arfeen Khan who have provided not only knowledge but also the inspiration to strive for excellence. Your guidance has been invaluable in helping me understand the power of values and the importance of character.

To my friends and colleagues, who have walked this path with me, sharing in both the challenges and triumphs. Your camaraderie and encouragement have been a constant source of strength.

To my family, whose love and belief in me have been the cornerstone of my success. Thank you for being my anchor and my biggest cheerleaders.

To all those who have touched my life in ways big and small, and have contributed to the person I am today. Your influence is reflected in every page of this book.

And finally, to my readers. May this book inspire you to fuel your life with the values that build true character and lead to lasting success. Remember, the journey of personal growth is ongoing, and the rewards of living a value-driven life are immeasurable.

Contents

Foreword

In an era where the race for material success and social validation often eclipses our deeper aspirations, it is rare to find a voice that calls us back to the core of our humanity. Krunal Shah is one such voice, and Life Without Fuel: Fueling Your Life with Values | Building Character for Lasting Success is a testament to the profound impact that living a value-driven life can have on our personal and professional fulfillment.

I first met Krunal Shah at a pivotal moment in my own journey, a time when I was grappling with the dissonance between outward achievements and inner contentment. It was through Krunal Shah's guidance and wisdom that I began to understand the essence of true success—one that is not measured by wealth or status, but by the strength of our character and the integrity of our actions.

This book is more than a guide; it is a beacon for those who seek to navigate the complexities of modern life with a steadfast commitment to values such as honesty, compassion, and perseverance. Krunal Shah eloquently articulates the importance of these principles, drawing from personal experiences, timeless wisdom, and the inspiring stories of others who have chosen to live by these ideals.

One of the most compelling aspects of this book is its practicality. Krunal Shah doesn't merely present abstract concepts; instead, he offers tangible strategies and actionable steps to help readers integrate these values into their daily lives. Whether you are at the beginning of your career, in the midst of personal challenges, or simply seeking a more meaningful path, this book provides the tools and insights needed to build a life of lasting success.

As you embark on this journey through the pages of Life Without Fuel, prepare to be challenged and inspired. You will be encouraged to look inward, to confront the habits and mindsets that may be holding you back, and to embrace a way of living that is both purposeful and fulfilling.

In a world that often prioritizes the fleeting and the superficial,Krunal Shah reminds us of the enduring power of values. He shows us that by fueling our lives with these principles, we can create not only personal success but also contribute to a more compassionate and just society.

It is with great admiration and respect that I introduce this transformative work. May it inspire you, as it has inspired me, to live a life without fuel but full of values, and to build a character that stands the test of time.

With heartfelt endorsement,
Riddhi Shah

Preface

In today's fast-paced world, where success is often measured by material wealth and superficial achievements, it's easy to lose sight of what truly matters. We find ourselves running on empty, fueled by external validation,more expectation and fleeting rewards. This book, Life Without Fuel: Fueling Your Life with Values | Building Character for Lasting Success, is a journey back to the basics—a call to rediscover the timeless values that form the bedrock of a fulfilling and meaningful life.

I embarked on this journey not from a place of theory, but from personal experience. Like many, I once believed that success was solely about reaching the next milestone, accumulating accolades, and outpacing the competition. Yet, despite outward successes, I felt a void, a nagging sense that something essential was missing. This realization set me on a path to explore deeper sources of fulfillment and lasting success.

Throughout this book, I share insights gained from my own life and the lives of those I've encountered—people who have taught me invaluable lessons about integrity, resilience, compassion, and authenticity. These stories and reflections aim to illustrate how living a value-driven life can transform not just our personal journeys, but also the world around us.

The essence of this book is simple yet profound: true success is rooted in strong character and unwavering values. It's about finding joy and purpose in who we are, not just in what we achieve. It's about understanding that life's inevitable ups and downs are opportunities for growth, shaping us into better, more compassionate individuals.

My hope is that this book will inspire you to look within, to fuel your life with values that build character, and to pursue a path of lasting success. Whether you are at the beginning of your journey or well along the way, may these pages offer guidance, encouragement, and a renewed sense of purpose.

Thank you for joining me on this journey. Life is beautiful, and every step—whether an uphill climb or a downhill coast—is part of the adventure. Embrace it with an open heart and a steadfast commitment to living a life without fuel, but full of values.

With gratitude,

Krunal Shah

Acknowledgements

Writing this book has been a journey of reflection, growth, and immense gratitude. I would like to take this opportunity to acknowledge the many individuals who have contributed to this endeavor.

First and foremost, I extend my deepest gratitude to my parents, whose unwavering love, support, and guidance have been the foundation of my values and character. Your teachings have been my guiding light and your example, my inspiration.

To my mentors,thank you for your wisdom and encouragement. Your insights have shaped my understanding of true success and the importance of living a value-driven life. Special thanks to Mr.Arfeen Khan for your invaluable vision,support and for pushing me to think deeper and aim higher.

To my friends and colleagues, thank you for your companionship and support. Your belief in me has been a constant source of motivation, and your shared experiences have enriched this book in countless ways.

To my family,especially wife Riddhi Shah, thank you for your patience and understanding throughout the Life adventures journey. Your love and encouragement have been my strength, especially during the challenging moments.

I am also deeply grateful to Notion Press, whose expertise and dedication have been instrumental in bringing this book to life. Thank you for believing in this project and for your meticulous attention to detail.

To the countless individuals whose stories and experiences have inspired the content of this book, thank you for sharing your journeys with me. Your courage and resilience are at the heart of this work.

Finally, to my readers, thank you for embarking on this journey with me. Your quest for personal growth and lasting success is the reason this book exists. May it inspire you to fuel your life with values and build a character that stands the test of time.

With heartfelt gratitude,
Krunal Shah

Prologue

In a world driven by rapid advancements and relentless pursuit of success, we often find ourselves caught in a cycle of constant motion. We chase after goals, accolades, and material possessions, believing they are the true markers of achievement. Yet, amidst this whirlwind, many of us experience a profound emptiness, a sense that something essential is missing.

This book, Life Without Fuel: Fueling Your Life with Values | Building Character for Lasting Success, is born out of the recognition that true fulfillment and lasting success are not found in the external rewards we so often seek. Instead, they lie within the core values that define who we are and how we live our lives.

My own journey of discovery began during a time of personal and professional turmoil. Despite outward success, I felt a deep sense of dissatisfaction and a lack of purpose. It was during this period of introspection that I realized the key to a meaningful life was not in achieving more, but in being more—more authentic, more compassionate, more resilient.

This book is a guide to living a life fueled by values, where character and integrity form the foundation of our actions and decisions. It is a call to shift our focus from the ephemeral to the enduring, from the superficial to the substantial. Through personal anecdotes, insights from influential figures, and practical advice, I aim to illuminate the path to a life of lasting success grounded in unwavering values.

The chapters ahead will explore the essence of key values such as honesty, empathy, perseverance, and gratitude. We will delve into how these values can transform our lives, our relationships, and our communities. By embracing these principles, we can navigate life's inevitable ups and downs with grace and purpose, finding beauty in every step of the journey.

As you read this book, I invite you to reflect on your own values and how they shape your life. Consider this an opportunity to realign with what truly matters, to build a character that withstands the test of time, and to achieve a success that is both meaningful and enduring.

Welcome to Life Without Fuel: Fueling Your Life with Values | Building Character for Lasting Success. May this journey inspire you to fuel your life with the values & strength that lead to true fulfillment and lasting success.

With warm regards,

Krunal Shah

ONE
MINDSET

A mindset is a set of beliefs, attitudes, and perceptions that shape how an individual interprets and responds to various situations and experiences. It encompasses one's cognitive framework and influences behaviors, decision-making processes, and overall approach to life challenges and opportunities.

There are generally two primary types of mindsets:

Fixed Mindset: This mindset is characterized by the belief that abilities and intelligence are static and unchangeable. Individuals with a fixed mindset tend to avoid challenges, give up easily when faced with obstacles, see effort as fruitless, and feel threatened by the success of others.

Growth Mindset: Coined by psychologist Carol Dweck, a growth mindset is the belief that abilities and intelligence can be developed through dedication, hard work, and learning. People with a growth mindset embrace challenges, persist in the face of setbacks, see effort as a path to mastery, learn from criticism, and find inspiration in others' successes.

A person's mindset significantly influences their motivation, resilience, and success in various aspects of life, including personal development, relationships, and professional endeavors.

The importance of having a great mindset cannot be overstated, as it significantly impacts various facets of an individual's personal and professional life. Here are some key reasons why a great mindset is crucial:

1.Resilience and Adaptability: A positive and growth-oriented mindset helps individuals bounce back from setbacks and adapt to changes more effectively. It fosters resilience, enabling people to cope with challenges and recover from failures.

2.Enhanced Problem-Solving Skills: A great mindset encourages innovative thinking and a solution-oriented approach. It allows individuals to view problems as opportunities for growth and development, leading to more effective and creative solutions.

3.Increased Motivation and Productivity: Individuals with a great mindset are more likely to stay motivated and focused on their goals. They are driven by the belief that effort and persistence will lead to success, which enhances their productivity.

4.Improved Relationships: A positive mindset promotes better communication, empathy, and understanding in relationships. It helps individuals approach interactions with an open and constructive attitude, leading to healthier and more fulfilling connections.

5.Greater Job Satisfaction and Career Success: A growth mindset encourages continuous learning and professional development. This attitude leads to greater job satisfaction, as individuals feel more competent and confident in their abilities, ultimately advancing their careers.

6.Better Stress Management: A great mindset equips individuals with the tools to manage stress and anxiety more effectively. It helps them maintain a balanced perspective and use stress as a motivator rather than a hindrance.

7.Higher Levels of Self-Efficacy: Believing in one's ability to achieve goals and overcome challenges is a hallmark of a great mindset. This self-efficacy boosts confidence and empowers individuals to take on new challenges and responsibilities.

8.Health and Well-Being: A positive mindset is linked to better physical and mental health. It reduces the risk of depression and anxiety, enhances immune function, and promotes overall well-being.

9.Leadership and Influence: Great leaders often possess a growth mindset, which allows them to inspire and motivate others. They lead by example, encouraging their teams to embrace challenges, learn from failures, and strive for continuous improvement.

10.Long-Term Success: Ultimately, a great mindset lays the foundation for sustained success in various life domains. It fosters a lifelong commitment to personal and professional growth, enabling individuals to achieve their full potential.

In summary, cultivating a great mindset is essential for achieving personal fulfillment, building strong relationships, excelling professionally, and maintaining overall well-being. It is a powerful tool that shapes how individuals approach and navigate life's challenges and opportunities.bility to improve and succeed. A professional who takes on challenging projects with the confidence that they can develop the necessary skills and knowledge demonstrates a great mindset.

Having a great mindset offers numerous benefits that can positively impact various aspects of an individual's life, from personal growth to professional success. Here are some key benefits:

1.Enhanced Resilience: A great mindset helps individuals bounce back from setbacks and failures, viewing them as learning opportunities rather than insurmountable obstacles.

2.Improved Problem-Solving: With a positive and growth-oriented mindset, individuals approach problems creatively and proactively, leading to more effective and innovative solutions.

3.Increased Motivation: A growth mindset fosters intrinsic motivation, driving individuals to set and pursue meaningful goals with determination and enthusiasm.

4.Greater Adaptability: Individuals with a great mindset are more open to change and flexible in their approaches, enabling them to thrive in dynamic and uncertain environments.

5.Better Stress Management: A positive mindset equips individuals with tools to manage stress and anxiety, helping them maintain a balanced and healthy perspective even under pressure.

6.Higher Productivity: With a focus on continuous improvement and efficiency, individuals with a great mindset tend to be more productive and effective in their tasks and responsibilities.

7.Enhanced Leadership Skills: Leaders with a great mindset inspire and motivate their teams, foster a culture of growth and learning, and lead by example.

8.Improved Relationships: A positive mindset promotes better communication, empathy, and understanding in personal and professional relationships, leading to stronger and more fulfilling connections.

9.Increased Job Satisfaction: By aligning personal growth with professional goals, individuals find greater fulfillment and satisfaction in their careers.

10.Continuous Learning and Development: A growth mindset encourages lifelong learning, ensuring that individuals constantly seek to acquire new skills and knowledge.

11.Higher Self-Esteem and Confidence: Believing in the ability to grow and improve enhances self-esteem and confidence, empowering individuals to take on new challenges.

12.Greater Creativity: A mindset that embraces challenges and views failures as learning opportunities fosters creative thinking and innovation.

13.Healthier Work-Life Balance: A positive mindset helps individuals set realistic goals and priorities, contributing to a better balance between work and personal life.

14.Stronger Team Dynamics: In a team setting, a great mindset encourages collaboration, mutual support, and collective problem-solving, enhancing overall team performance.

15.Better Conflict Resolution: With a growth mindset, individuals approach conflicts constructively, seeking to understand different perspectives and find mutually beneficial solutions.

16.Goal Achievement: A focus on growth and improvement helps individuals set and achieve ambitious yet realistic goals, leading to personal and professional success.

17.Positive Influence on Others: Individuals with a great mindset often serve as role models, positively influencing and inspiring those around them to adopt similar attitudes and behaviors.

18.Greater Sense of Purpose: A positive mindset helps individuals align their actions with their values and long-term goals, leading to a deeper sense of purpose and direction.

19.Optimized Performance: Continuous improvement and learning lead to peak performance in various domains, from sports and academics to business and personal endeavors.

20.Overall Well-Being: A great mindset contributes to better mental and emotional health, reducing the risk of depression and anxiety and promoting a general sense of well-being

While a positive or growth mindset is generally beneficial, there can be potential disadvantages or challenges associated with it if not approached or applied correctly. Here are some potential downsides:

1. Overemphasis on Positivity

Ignoring Negative Emotions: A constant focus on positivity can lead to suppression of negative emotions, which are important for processing experiences and achieving emotional balance.

Toxic Positivity: This occurs when the emphasis on positive thinking dismisses legitimate feelings of sadness or frustration, leading to feelings of isolation or inadequacy.

2. Unrealistic Expectations

Overconfidence: Believing that you can achieve anything simply through effort might lead to overestimating your abilities and taking on tasks beyond your capacity.

Frustration and Burnout: Setting unrealistic goals can result in disappointment and burnout if the desired results aren't achieved despite significant effort.

3. Misinterpreting Feedback

Misunderstanding Constructive Criticism: Overly focusing on maintaining a positive mindset might cause you to misinterpret constructive feedback as negativity, thereby missing opportunities for genuine improvement.

Ignoring Red Flags: An over-optimistic outlook might lead to ignoring important warning signs or red flags in various situations, whether in personal relationships or professional settings.

4. External Pressure

Social Pressure: Feeling pressured to always maintain a positive or growth mindset can be stressful and lead to guilt or shame when you're not able to maintain that outlook.

Comparisons: Comparing your mindset progress with others can create unnecessary stress and feelings of inadequacy.

5. Neglecting Practical Constraints

Underestimating Structural Challenges: Believing that a positive mindset can overcome all obstacles might lead to underestimating systemic or structural challenges that require more than individual effort to address.

Resource Misallocation: Focusing too much on mindset improvements might cause neglect of other practical aspects of personal or professional development, such as skill-building or networking.

6. Ignoring Individual Differences

One-Size-Fits-All Approach: Not everyone responds to mindset interventions in the same way. Overgeneralizing the benefits of a growth mindset can ignore individual differences in personality, circumstances, and mental health.

7. Short-Term Focus

Immediate Gratification: A focus on short-term mindset changes might overlook the importance of long-term strategies and perseverance needed to achieve significant, lasting results.

8. Cultural Context

Cultural Misalignment: Mindset concepts developed in one cultural context may not easily translate or be applicable in another, leading to misunderstandings or ineffective application of those principles.

9. Blaming the Individual

Victim-Blaming: Promoting the idea that mindset is the primary factor in success can lead to blaming individuals for their circumstances, ignoring external factors such as socio-economic conditions, discrimination, or access to resources.

In summary, while developing a positive or growth mindset has many advantages, it is important to apply these concepts thoughtfully and in balance with other factors. Being aware of potential disadvantages helps in using mindset strategies more effectively and compassionately

Great mindset can be seen through various attitudes, behaviors, and approaches that individuals exhibit in different situations. Here are some illustrative examples:

Embracing Challenges: Viewing challenges as opportunities for growth rather than obstacles. For instance, a student who finds a subject difficult but approaches it with the determination to learn and improve exemplifies a great mindset.

Learning from Criticism: Welcoming constructive feedback and using it to improve. An employee who actively seeks feedback from their manager and colleagues, and then implements suggestions to enhance their performance, demonstrates a growth mindset.

Persistence: Showing resilience and determination in the face of setbacks. An entrepreneur who experiences multiple business failures but continues to innovate and pursue new ventures embodies a great mindset.

Adaptability: Being open to change and flexible in different circumstances. A professional who embraces new technologies and adapts to changing industry trends to stay relevant displays a great mindset.

Continuous Learning: Committing to lifelong learning and self-improvement. An individual who regularly takes courses, reads books, and seeks new knowledge to enhance their skills and understanding showcases a growth mindset.

Positive Attitude: Maintaining a positive outlook even in challenging situations. A team leader who stays optimistic during tough projects and motivates their team to keep pushing forward highlights a great mindset.

Taking Responsibility: Owning up to mistakes and learning from them rather than blaming others. A manager who admits a project's shortcomings, analyzes what went wrong, and devises a plan to prevent similar issues in the future demonstrates a growth mindset.

Empathy and Understanding: Showing empathy towards others and understanding different perspectives. A colleague who listens actively and tries to understand team members' viewpoints to resolve conflicts effectively embodies a great mindset.

Setting and Achieving Goals: Setting ambitious yet achievable goals and working diligently towards them. An athlete who sets a personal best record to beat and trains consistently to achieve it reflects a growth mindset.

Innovation: Encouraging creativity and innovation in problem-solving. A software developer who experiments with new coding techniques and learns from both successes and failures exemplifies a great mindset.

Balanced View of Success and Failure: Viewing success as a result of effort and failure as a learning experience. A student who celebrates their successes but also critically assesses their failures to learn and improve highlights a growth mindset.

Self-Belief and Confidence: Believing in one's ability to improve and succeed. A professional who takes on challenging projects with the confidence that they can develop the necessary skills and knowledge demonstrates a great mindset.

Collaboration: Valuing teamwork and learning from others. A project manager who fosters a collaborative environment where team members share knowledge and skills exhibits a great mindset.

Seeking Opportunities: Actively looking for opportunities to grow and develop. A mid-level executive who volunteers for cross-functional projects to gain broader experience showcases a growth mindset.

Vision and Purpose: Having a clear vision and purpose that drives one's actions. A non-profit leader who is driven by the mission to make a positive impact in the community, continuously finding ways to enhance their organization's effectiveness, exemplifies a great mindset.

These examples illustrate how a great mindset can manifest in various aspects of life, driving individuals towards continuous improvement, resilience, and success.

Improving one's mindset involves adopting positive habits, challenging negative thoughts, and continuously working on personal growth. Here are some strategies to help enhance your mindset:

1. Cultivate a Growth Mindset

Embrace Challenges: View challenges as opportunities to learn and grow.

Learn from Criticism: Use constructive criticism to improve yourself.

Persistence: Keep trying even when things get tough.

2. Practice Gratitude

Daily Gratitude Journal: Write down things you are thankful for every day.

Appreciate Small Things: Take time to notice and appreciate the small joys in life.

3. Positive Self-Talk

Affirmations: Use positive affirmations to boost your self-esteem.

Reframe Negative Thoughts: When you catch yourself thinking negatively, try to reframe those thoughts in a positive light.

4. Surround Yourself with Positive Influences

Supportive Network: Spend time with people who uplift and support you.

Limit Negative Media: Reduce exposure to negative news and social media.

5. Set Goals and Take Action

SMART Goals: Set Specific, Measurable, Achievable, Relevant, and Time-bound goals.

Action Plan: Create a step-by-step plan to achieve your goals and take consistent action.

6. Mindfulness and Meditation

Daily Practice: Incorporate mindfulness or meditation into your daily routine to help manage stress and improve focus.

Mindful Activities: Engage in activities that promote mindfulness, such as yoga or deep breathing exercises.

7. Continuous Learning

Read Books: Read books on personal development, psychology, and self-help.

Online Courses: Take courses or attend workshops to learn new skills and expand your knowledge.

8. Healthy Lifestyle

Exercise Regularly: Physical activity boosts mood and reduces anxiety.

Balanced Diet: Eat a healthy, balanced diet to fuel your body and mind.

Adequate Sleep: Ensure you get enough sleep to maintain cognitive function and emotional well-being.

9. Reflect and Adjust

Regular Reflection: Take time to reflect on your progress and identify areas for improvement.

Adaptability: Be willing to adjust your strategies and goals as needed.

10. Seek Professional Help if Needed Coaching: Consider working with a life coach to address deeper issues and receive personalized guidance.

By consistently applying these strategies, you can gradually shift your mindset towards a more positive, resilient, and growth-oriented perspective.

Many celebrities exemplify a great mindset through their resilience, positive attitudes, and continuous growth. Here are a few notable examples:

1. Oprah Winfrey

Resilience and Growth: Oprah's rise from a challenging childhood to becoming one of the most influential media moguls showcases her resilience and growth mindset. She often speaks about the importance of self-belief, education, and continuous self-improvement.

Quotes: "Turn your wounds into wisdom." "The greatest discovery of all time is that a person can change his future by merely changing his attitude."

2. Dwayne "The Rock" Johnson

Work Ethic and Positivity: Known for his incredible work ethic and positive outlook, Dwayne Johnson emphasizes the importance of hard work, perseverance, and maintaining a positive attitude even in the face of adversity.

Quotes: "Be humble. Be hungry. And always be the hardest worker in the room." "Success isn't always about 'greatness.' It's about consistency."

3. J.K. Rowling

Perseverance and Belief: Before achieving immense success with the Harry Potter series, J.K. Rowling faced numerous rejections and personal hardships. Her story is a testament to the power of perseverance and self-belief.

Quotes: "Rock bottom became the solid foundation on which I rebuilt my life." "It is impossible to live without failing at something, unless you live so cautiously that you might as well not have lived at all."

4. Michael Jordan

Failure as a Learning Tool: Michael Jordan, considered one of the greatest basketball players of all time, has often spoken about how his failures and setbacks fueled his success and growth.

Quotes: "I've missed more than 9,000 shots in my career. I've lost almost 300 games. Twenty-six times I've been trusted to take the game-winning shot and missed. I've failed over and over and over again in my life. And that is why I succeed."

5. Serena Williams

Determination and Resilience: Serena Williams' career in tennis is marked by her determination, resilience, and continuous striving for excellence despite facing numerous challenges.

Quotes: "I am lucky that whatever fear I have inside me, my desire to win is always stronger." "I really think a champion is defined not by their wins but by how they can recover when they fall."

6. Elon Musk

Innovation and Risk-Taking: Elon Musk, known for his ventures like Tesla and SpaceX, exemplifies a growth mindset through his willingness to take risks, embrace failure, and continuously innovate.

Quotes: "Failure is an option here. If things are not failing, you are not innovating enough." "When something is important enough, you do it even if the odds are not in your favor."

7. Michelle Obama

Empowerment and Positivity: Michelle Obama emphasizes the importance of education, empowerment, and maintaining a positive attitude. Her initiatives and public speaking often focus on inspiring others to reach their full potential.

Quotes: "You may not always have a comfortable life and you will not always be able to solve all of the world's problems at once but don't ever underestimate the importance you can have because history has shown us that courage can be contagious and hope can take on a life of its own." "Success is only meaningful and enjoyable if it feels like your own."

TWO
SIGNIFICANCE

Significance refers to the importance, relevance, or meaningfulness of something within a specific context. It indicates the value or impact that something holds, whether it's a concept, event, action, or object. Understanding the significance of something involves recognizing its implications, consequences, or contributions to a larger purpose, goal, or understanding. In essence, significance provides insight into the value or importance of something within a given context, helping to inform decisions, interpretations, and evaluations.

"Significance" is basically about how important something is in a certain situation. It's like saying, "This thing really matters because of what it means or what it does." It's like realizing why something is a big deal or why it's worth paying attention to. For example, when you understand the significance of an event, you get why it's so important in history or why it matters so much to people. It's like seeing the deeper meaning or impact behind something.

The importance of significance lies in its ability to provide context, clarity, and direction in various aspects of life. Here are some key reasons why significance is important:

1. Guidance in Decision-Making: Understanding the significance of different options helps individuals and organizations make informed decisions aligned with their goals, values, and priorities. It provides a framework for evaluating choices and determining the most meaningful course of action.

2. Motivation and Purpose: Recognizing the significance of goals, actions, or experiences can motivate individuals to pursue them with greater enthusiasm and commitment. It instills a sense of purpose and meaning,

fueling perseverance and resilience in the face of challenges.

3. Effective Communication: Significance enhances communication by providing a shared understanding of why something matters. It enables individuals to convey the importance of their ideas, initiatives, or concerns more effectively, fostering collaboration and alignment among stakeholders.

4. Positive Impact: Understanding the significance of one's actions or contributions allows individuals to focus their efforts on areas where they can make the most meaningful impact. It encourages them to prioritize activities that benefit others and contribute to the greater good.

5. Personal Fulfillment: Engaging in activities or pursuits that hold significance can lead to a greater sense of fulfillment and satisfaction. It allows individuals to connect with their values, passions, and aspirations, leading to a more meaningful and rewarding life.

6. Resilience and Adaptability: Recognizing the significance of challenges or setbacks helps individuals develop resilience and adaptability in navigating life's ups and downs. It encourages them to approach obstacles as opportunities for growth and learning, rather than insurmountable barriers.

7. Relationship Building: Significance strengthens relationships by fostering mutual understanding, respect, and appreciation among individuals. It encourages empathy and compassion, leading to deeper connections and more meaningful interactions with others.

8. Alignment of Efforts: Understanding the significance of shared goals or values promotes alignment and cooperation among team members, organizations, or communities. It facilitates collaboration towards common objectives, maximizing collective impact and effectiveness.

9. Ethical Decision-Making: Significance prompts individuals to consider the broader implications of their choices and actions, including ethical and moral considerations. It encourages responsible decision-making that takes into account the well-being of others and the long-term consequences of one's behavior.

10. Legacy and Impact: Recognizing the significance of one's contributions can inspire individuals to leave a lasting legacy and make a positive impact on future generations. It motivates them to strive for excellence and pursue endeavors that leave the world a better place than they found it.

Overall, the importance of significance lies in its ability to guide, motivate, and inspire individuals to lead more purposeful, fulfilling lives while making meaningful contributions to society and the world at large.

To increase the significance of something, you can consider the following steps:

1. Define Clear Objectives: Clearly define what you want to achieve or the purpose you want to serve. Having clear objectives helps you understand why something is important and what impact it can have.

2. Identify Key Stakeholders: Identify the people or groups who are affected by or have a stake in the matter. Understanding their perspectives and needs can help you better appreciate the significance of the issue.

3. Highlight Benefits: Emphasize the benefits or positive outcomes associated with the matter. Show how it can make a difference or add value to people's lives.

4. Communicate Effectively: Use clear and persuasive communication to convey the significance of the issue to others. Tailor your message to your audience and use compelling arguments or examples to make your case.

5. Seek Support: Build alliances and seek support from others who share your goals or values. Working together can amplify the significance of the issue and increase its impact.

6. Take Action: Take concrete actions to address the issue or achieve your objectives. Action speaks louder than words and can demonstrate the significance of the matter more effectively than just talking about it.

7. Measure Impact: Monitor and evaluate the impact of your efforts to assess the significance of the issue. Collect data, gather feedback, and track progress to understand how your actions are making a difference.

8. Adapt and Improve: Continuously adapt and improve your approach based on feedback and results. Be open to new ideas and approaches that can enhance the significance of the issue and increase its impact over time.

By following these steps, you can increase the significance of the issue or matter you are focused on and maximize its impact on the people and communities it affects.

Understanding the significance of something brings several benefits:

1. Clarity of Purpose: Recognizing the significance of a goal or action provides clarity of purpose, helping individuals and organizations understand why it matters and what they are working towards.

2. Motivation and Inspiration: Knowing the significance of their efforts can motivate individuals to stay committed and inspired, even in the face of

challenges or setbacks.

3. Informed Decision-Making: Understanding the significance of different options or choices enables informed decision-making, allowing individuals to prioritize activities that align with their goals and values.

4. Enhanced Satisfaction: Engaging in activities that hold significance can lead to a greater sense of satisfaction and fulfillment, as individuals feel that their efforts are meaningful and impactful.

5. Positive Impact: Recognizing the significance of their actions can inspire individuals to make positive contributions to their communities, organizations, or society as a whole, leading to tangible benefits for others.

6. Resilience: Understanding the significance of their goals or values can help individuals develop resilience and perseverance, enabling them to overcome obstacles and challenges with determination and optimism.

7. Personal Growth: Reflecting on the significance of their experiences and accomplishments can foster personal growth and development, encouraging individuals to learn from their successes and failures alike.

8. Stronger Relationships: Recognizing the significance of others' contributions and perspectives promotes mutual respect and understanding, fostering stronger and more collaborative relationships.

9. Alignment of Efforts: Understanding the significance of shared goals or values facilitates alignment among team members, enabling them to work together effectively towards a common purpose.

10. Long-Term Impact: Recognizing the significance of their actions encourages individuals to consider the long-term implications of their decisions, leading to more sustainable and responsible choices.

Overall, understanding the significance of something provides a framework for meaningful action, fostering motivation, resilience, and positive impact in various aspects of life.

While significance typically brings numerous benefits, there can also be potential disadvantages or challenges associated with it in certain situations.

Here are some possible drawbacks:

1. Overemphasis: Focusing excessively on the significance of something may lead to tunnel vision or narrow-mindedness, where individuals or organizations become fixated on specific goals, ideas, or outcomes at the expense of considering alternative perspectives or possibilities.

2. Resistance to Change: Perceiving something as significant may create resistance to change, as individuals or groups may be reluctant to deviate

from established practices or beliefs that they perceive as important or valuable.

3. Misinterpretation: Different individuals or groups may interpret the significance of something differently based on their own biases, perspectives, or interests. This can lead to misunderstandings, conflicts, or miscommunication when attempting to convey the importance of a particular concept, event, or idea.

4. Inflexibility: Perceiving something as significant may lead to rigidity or inflexibility in thinking and behavior, as individuals or organizations may be less willing to adapt or compromise in response to changing circumstances or new information.

5. Selective Attention: Focusing solely on the significance of certain aspects or factors may result in overlooking or neglecting other important considerations that could have significant implications. This selective attention can lead to blind spots or missed opportunities for growth and improvement.

6. Pressure to Perform: Perceiving something as significant may create pressure to perform or meet high expectations, leading to stress, anxiety, or burnout among individuals or teams striving to achieve or maintain the perceived level of significance.

7. Dependency: Relying too heavily on the significance of certain individuals, resources, or systems may create dependency and vulnerability, as disruptions or changes to those significant factors could have cascading effects on the overall functioning or stability of an organization or system.

8. Complacency: Perceiving something as significant may breed complacency or overconfidence, as individuals or organizations may assume that their current approach or status quo is inherently valuable or superior, leading to stagnation or missed opportunities for innovation and improvement.

9. Short-Term Thinking: Focusing exclusively on the significance of short-term gains or outcomes may lead to neglecting long-term sustainability or ethical considerations, resulting in decisions or actions that prioritize immediate benefits at the expense of broader consequences or responsibilities.

10. Exclusion: Perceiving something as significant may inadvertently exclude or marginalize alternative perspectives, voices, or experiences that are not deemed as significant by those in positions of power or influence, perpetuating inequality or discrimination.

While significance can bring numerous benefits, it's essential to recognize and mitigate these potential disadvantages to ensure balanced decision-making, inclusivity, and adaptability in personal, professional, and societal contexts.

Significance can vary widely depending on the context, but here are a few common examples:

1. Historical Events: Significant historical events, such as the signing of the Declaration of Independence, the fall of the Berlin Wall, or the moon landing, have had profound impacts on societies and shaped the course of history.

2. Scientific Discoveries: Breakthrough scientific discoveries, like the theory of relativity by Albert Einstein or the discovery of penicillin by Alexander Fleming, have revolutionized our understanding of the universe and transformed modern medicine.

3. Cultural Movements: Cultural movements, such as the Civil Rights Movement in the United States or the Women's Suffrage Movement, have sparked social change and challenged long standing norms and inequalities.

4. Literary Works: Classic literary works, such as Shakespeare's plays or Orwell's "1984," have had enduring significance, shaping literature, language, and culture for generations.

5. Inventions and Innovations: Inventions and innovations, like the printing press, the internet, or the smartphone, have dramatically altered the way we communicate, work, and live our lives.

6. Natural Phenomena: Natural phenomena, such as solar eclipses or volcanic eruptions, hold significance for scientists, historians, and cultures around the world, often inspiring awe and fascination.

7. Personal Milestones: Personal milestones, such as graduations, weddings, or the birth of a child, hold significant meaning for individuals and families, marking important transitions and achievements in life.

8. Symbolic Gestures: Symbolic gestures, such as the raising of a flag or the lighting of a candle, can hold deep significance in commemorating events, honoring individuals, or expressing solidarity and unity.

9. Artistic Creations: Masterpieces of art, music, or film, like Leonardo da Vinci's "Mona Lisa," Beethoven's Ninth Symphony, or Spielberg's "Schindler's List," have significant cultural and artistic value, resonating with audiences across time and space.

10. Global Issues: Global issues, such as climate change, poverty, or human rights abuses, hold significance for humanity as a whole,

challenging us to address pressing challenges and work towards a more equitable and sustainable future.

These examples illustrate the diverse range of phenomena and experiences that can hold significance, shaping our understanding of the world and influencing our actions and decisions.

When Oprah Winfrey announces a new book club selection, it significantly impacts the literary world. Oprah's book club has a long-standing reputation for promoting meaningful and impactful reads, often resulting in a significant boost in sales and recognition for the selected authors. The Oprah Book Club seal of approval holds considerable significance for both established and emerging writers, as it can lead to increased visibility, book sales, and critical acclaim. Additionally, Oprah's influence extends beyond the literary sphere, as her recommendations often spark conversations and inspire readers worldwide, highlighting the significance of her cultural impact and authority as a tastemaker.

In summary, significance plays a fundamental role in shaping our perceptions, decisions, and overall quality of life. By recognizing and embracing what holds significance to us, we can lead more fulfilling, purpose-driven lives and make meaningful contributions to the world around us.

Improving the significance of something involves enhancing its importance, relevance, or impact within a particular context. Here are some strategies to improve significance:

1. Clarify Goals and Objectives: Clearly define the goals and objectives associated with the subject matter to ensure alignment with broader purposes or priorities. Understanding the overarching objectives can help identify why the subject matter is significant and how it contributes to larger goals.

2. Highlight Key Contributions: Identify and emphasize the specific contributions or implications of the subject matter, highlighting its importance and relevance to stakeholders or decision-makers. Focus on the value it brings and how it addresses key needs, challenges, or opportunities.

3. Provide Context: Offer context or background information to help stakeholders understand the significance of the subject matter within its broader historical, social, or organizational context. Explain how it fits into larger trends, patterns, or initiatives.

4. Demonstrate Impact: Provide evidence or examples that illustrate the tangible impact or outcomes associated with the subject matter. Show how

it has made a difference, solved problems, or achieved positive results in the past or could do so in the future.

5. Engage Stakeholders: Involve relevant stakeholders in discussions about the significance of the subject matter, seeking their perspectives, feedback, and buy-in. Engaging stakeholders can help ensure that their interests and concerns are addressed, enhancing the perceived significance of the subject matter.

6. Communicate Effectively: Use clear, concise, and compelling communication strategies to convey the significance of the subject matter to various audiences. Tailor messages resonate with the interests, values, and priorities of different stakeholders, making the case for its importance in a persuasive manner.

7. Seek Recognition: Pursue opportunities to showcase the significance of the subject matter through recognition, awards, or accolades. Highlighting achievements or successes can raise awareness and validate its importance in the eyes of others.

8. Continuously Evaluate and Improve: Regularly assess the significance of the subject matter in light of changing circumstances, needs, or priorities. Solicit feedback, monitor performance metrics, and adapt strategies as needed to ensure ongoing relevance and impact.

9. Promote Collaboration: Foster collaboration and partnerships with other individuals or organizations that share an interest in the subject matter. Pooling resources, expertise, and perspectives can enhance the significance of collective efforts and amplify their impact.

10. Encourage Innovation: Encourage creativity and innovation in exploring new ways to enhance the significance of the subject matter. Embrace experimentation, pilot projects, and iterative improvements to uncover new opportunities for growth and advancement.

By implementing these strategies, individuals and organizations can effectively enhance the significance of their initiatives, projects, or endeavors, thereby maximizing their impact and value within their respective contexts.

Improving the significance of something involves honing skills related to communication, strategic thinking, and stakeholder engagement. Here are some skills to develop to enhance the significance of a subject matter:

1. Communication Skills: Develop the ability to articulate the importance and relevance of the subject matter clearly and persuasively. Practice crafting compelling messages tailored to different audiences, using

language and examples that resonate with their interests and priorities.

2. Strategic Thinking: Cultivate strategic thinking skills to identify opportunities to enhance the significance of the subject matter within its broader context. Analyze trends, anticipate future needs or challenges, and develop strategies to position the subject matter as a valuable contributor to larger goals or objectives.

3. Research and Analysis: Strengthen research and analytical skills to gather relevant data, evidence, and insights that support the significance of the subject matter. Use critical thinking and problem-solving skills to interpret findings and draw meaningful conclusions about its impact and implications.

4. Stakeholder Engagement: Develop the ability to engage with stakeholders effectively to understand their perspectives, needs, and priorities related to the subject matter. Build relationships, solicit feedback, and collaborate with stakeholders to ensure their voices are heard and their interests are addressed.

5. Storytelling: Master the art of storytelling to convey the significance of the subject matter in a compelling and memorable way. Use narratives, anecdotes, and visuals to illustrate its impact, highlight key achievements, and inspire others to action.

6. Strategic Planning: Learn how to develop strategic plans and initiatives that leverage the significance of the subject matter to achieve broader goals or objectives. Set clear objectives, identify key milestones, and allocate resources effectively to maximize impact and value.

7. Adaptability: Cultivate adaptability and flexibility to respond to changing circumstances, needs, or priorities that may affect the significance of the subject matter. Embrace innovation, experimentation, and continuous improvement to stay relevant and impactful over time.

8. Networking: Build a strong professional network of individuals and organizations that can support and amplify the significance of the subject matter. Seek out opportunities for collaboration, partnership, and knowledge sharing to expand its reach and influence.

9. Leadership: Develop leadership skills to inspire others and drive positive change related to the subject matter. Lead by example, empower others to contribute, and foster a culture of innovation, collaboration, and accountability that reinforces its significance.

10. Evaluation and Reflection: Establish processes for evaluating and reflecting on the significance of the subject matter regularly. Monitor

progress, measure impact, and solicit feedback to identify strengths, weaknesses, and areas for improvement, and adapt strategies accordingly.

By developing these skills, individuals and organizations can effectively enhance the significance of their initiatives, projects, or endeavors, thereby maximizing their impact and value within their respective contexts.

An example of significance could be the development of a new medical treatment for a previously untreatable disease. This breakthrough could have significant implications in several ways:

1. Health Impact: The new treatment could significantly improve the health and well-being of individuals affected by the disease, potentially saving lives, reducing suffering, and improving quality of life for patients and their families.

2. Scientific Advancement: The development of the treatment represents a significant scientific advancement, pushing the boundaries of medical knowledge and technology. It opens up new possibilities for future research and innovation in the field of medicine.

3. Economic Implications: The successful development and commercialization of the treatment could have significant economic implications, creating opportunities for pharmaceutical companies, healthcare providers, and other related industries. It may generate revenue, create jobs, and stimulate economic growth in communities where it is produced and used.

4. Social and Cultural Impact: The availability of the treatment could have significant social and cultural implications, changing how the disease is perceived and treated within society. It may reduce stigma, increase awareness, and promote acceptance and inclusivity for individuals affected by the disease.

5. Global Health: The widespread adoption of the treatment could have significant implications for global health, particularly in regions where the disease is prevalent or resources for healthcare are limited. It may contribute to efforts to reduce health disparities, promote equity, and improve health outcomes on a global scale.

Overall, the development of a new medical treatment for a previously untreatable disease exemplifies significance by addressing pressing health needs, advancing scientific knowledge, stimulating economic growth, promoting social and cultural change, and improving global health outcomes.

The significance of various aspects in life holds immense importance as it influences our perceptions, decisions, and overall well-being. Here's why significance is crucial in life:

1. Guidance in Decision Making: Understanding the significance of different options helps us make informed decisions aligned with our values, goals, and priorities. It guides us towards choices that are meaningful and beneficial for our personal and professional growth.

2. Motivation and Purpose: Recognizing the significance of our goals, aspirations, and actions provides us with motivation and purpose in life. It fuels our drive to pursue meaningful endeavors, overcome challenges, and strive for excellence.

3. Sense of Direction: Significance helps us navigate through life by providing a sense of direction and clarity about what truly matters to us. It enables us to focus our energy and resources on pursuits that align with our passions, values, and long-term objectives.

4. Enhanced Satisfaction and Fulfillment: Engaging in activities and relationships that hold significance to us brings a sense of satisfaction and fulfillment. It allows us to experience joy, contentment, and a deeper sense of meaning in our daily lives.

5. Resilience in Adversity: Understanding the significance of our experiences, setbacks, and challenges helps us cultivate resilience and strength in the face of adversity. It enables us to find purpose and meaning even in difficult circumstances, fostering growth and resilience.

6. Healthy Relationships: Recognizing the significance of our relationships fosters trust, mutual respect, and emotional connection with others. It encourages open communication, empathy, and support, leading to more fulfilling and harmonious relationships.

7. Personal Growth and Development: Significance plays a crucial role in our personal growth and development by encouraging self-reflection, introspection, and continuous learning. It motivates us to expand our horizons, explore new opportunities, and unleash our full potential.

8. Contributions to Society: Understanding the significance of our contributions to society inspires us to make a positive impact and leave a meaningful legacy. It drives us to engage in acts of kindness, service, and social responsibility, thereby enriching the lives of others and creating a better world.

9. Emotional Well-being: Recognizing the significance of our emotions, thoughts, and experiences promotes emotional well-being and resilience.

It encourages us to prioritize self-care, seek support when needed, and cultivate a positive outlook on life.

10. Legacy and Longevity: Significance allows us to create a lasting legacy and leave behind a positive imprint on the world. It ensures that our actions, values, and contributions continue to inspire and impact future generations long after we're gone.

In summary, significance plays a fundamental role in shaping our perceptions, decisions, and overall quality of life. By recognizing and embracing what holds significance to us, we can lead more fulfilling, purpose-driven lives and make meaningful contributions to the world around us.

THREE
RESPECT

CHAPTER 3 : Respect

Respect is a fundamental concept that encompasses admiration, consideration, and esteem for oneself and others. It involves recognizing the inherent worth, dignity, and rights of individuals, and treating them with courtesy, kindness, and fairness.

Key aspects of respect include:

1. Recognition: Acknowledging the value, worth, and uniqueness of oneself and others. Respect involves recognizing the inherent dignity and rights of every individual, regardless of differences in background, beliefs, or status.

2. Consideration: Being considerate of others' feelings, perspectives, and boundaries. Respect involves taking the time to listen actively, empathize with others, and consider their needs and preferences in interactions and decisions.

3. Courtesy: Demonstrating politeness, kindness, and civility in interactions with others. Respect involves using polite language, showing appreciation, and treating others with courtesy and respect, even in challenging situations.

4. Empathy: Understanding and empathizing with the experiences, emotions, and challenges of others. Respect involves putting oneself in another person's shoes, seeking to understand their perspectives, and showing compassion and understanding.

5. Acceptance: Respecting the diversity and differences among individuals and embracing inclusivity and tolerance. Respect involves accepting others for who they are, without judgment or discrimination, and celebrating the richness of human diversity.

6. Boundaries: Respecting personal and professional boundaries and exercising restraint in behavior and interactions. Respect involves honoring others' privacy, autonomy, and consent, and refraining from actions that could cause harm or discomfort.

7. Reciprocity: Treating others as you would like to be treated yourself. Respect involves practicing the golden rule of treating others with the same kindness, consideration, and fairness that you would expect for yourself.

Overall, respect is a fundamental value that promotes positive relationships, fosters mutual understanding and cooperation, and contributes to a culture of dignity, fairness, and inclusivity in personal, professional, and societal contexts.

Respect brings numerous benefits to individuals, relationships, organizations, and society as a whole. Here are some of the key benefits of respect:

1. Positive Relationships: Respect forms the foundation of positive and healthy relationships. When individuals respect each other's opinions, feelings, and boundaries, it fosters trust, understanding, and mutual support in personal, professional, and social interactions.

2. Enhanced Communication: Respectful communication promotes open dialogue, active listening, and constructive feedback. When people communicate respectfully, it leads to clearer understanding, reduced conflicts, and more effective problem-solving.

3. Increased Collaboration: Respect encourages collaboration and teamwork among individuals with diverse perspectives and backgrounds. When people respect each other's contributions and viewpoints, it fosters cooperation, innovation, and creativity in achieving common goals.

4. Improved Morale and Engagement: A culture of respect enhances morale and engagement in organizations. When employees feel respected and valued for their contributions, they are more motivated, committed, and satisfied in their work, leading to higher productivity and retention rates.

5. Conflict Resolution: Respectful behavior facilitates conflict resolution and mediation. When individuals approach conflicts with respect and empathy, it promotes constructive dialogue, negotiation, and compromise, leading to mutually acceptable solutions and stronger relationships.

6. Stronger Leadership: Respectful leaders inspire trust, loyalty, and commitment among their followers. When leaders demonstrate respect for their team members' ideas, perspectives, and contributions, it fosters a

culture of trust, empowerment, and accountability within organizations.

7. Enhanced Well-Being: Respectful environments contribute to greater well-being and satisfaction among individuals. When people feel respected and valued by others, it boosts their self-esteem, confidence, and overall sense of belonging and fulfillment.

8. Promotion of Diversity and Inclusion: Respect promotes diversity and inclusion by valuing and embracing differences among individuals. When people respect each other's cultural backgrounds, identities, and perspectives, it creates a more inclusive and equitable society where everyone feels valued and respected.

9. Positive Reputation: Respectful behavior enhances one's reputation and image in personal and professional settings. When individuals are known for their respectful conduct and interactions, it builds trust, credibility, and goodwill among peers, colleagues, and the community.

10. Social Harmony: Respect fosters social harmony and cohesion by promoting tolerance, acceptance, and empathy. When people respect each other's rights, freedoms, and differences, it creates a harmonious and inclusive society where individuals can coexist peacefully and thrive together.

In summary, respect brings a multitude of benefits, including positive relationships, enhanced communication, increased collaboration, improved morale and engagement, effective conflict resolution, stronger leadership, enhanced well-being, promotion of diversity and inclusion, positive reputation, and social harmony. Cultivating respect is essential for building a more compassionate, equitable, and thriving world for everyone.

While respect is generally regarded as a positive attribute that fosters positive relationships and interactions, there can be potential disadvantages or challenges associated with it in certain situations. Here are a few possible disadvantages of respect:

1. Exploitation: In some cases, individuals may exploit others' respect for them for personal gain or manipulation. This can occur when someone takes advantage of the trust and goodwill of others to manipulate or control them, leading to unfair or harmful outcomes.

2. Unbalanced Relationships: Excessive respect or deference towards authority figures or individuals in positions of power can lead to unbalanced or unequal relationships. In such cases, one party may have undue influence or control over the other, leading to issues of dependency or subordination.

3. Unwarranted Compliance: Excessive respect for authority or tradition may result in blind obedience or conformity to norms or rules that are unjust or harmful. This can stifle critical thinking, creativity, and innovation, and perpetuate unfair or discriminatory practices.

4. Lack of Assertiveness: Overly respectful behavior may prevent individuals from expressing their own opinions, needs, or boundaries assertively. This can lead to feelings of resentment, frustration, or powerlessness, and inhibit healthy communication and collaboration.

5. Tolerance of Disrespect: In some cases, an emphasis on respect may lead individuals to tolerate disrespectful behavior from others, either out of fear of conflict or a desire to maintain harmony. This can perpetuate a cycle of disrespect and undermine efforts to foster positive relationships and environments.

6. Barriers to Change: Excessive respect for tradition or authority may create barriers to change or innovation, as individuals may be hesitant to challenge established norms or practices. This can hinder progress and adaptation in response to evolving needs or challenges.

7. Misplaced Priorities: Prioritizing respect above all else may sometimes lead to the neglect or compromise of other important values or principles, such as justice, fairness, or honesty. In such cases, the pursuit of respect may come at the expense of ethical integrity or moral responsibility.

8. Inequality: Respect can sometimes be unevenly distributed or withheld based on factors such as race, gender, or social status, leading to inequalities or discrimination. This can perpetuate systems of oppression or marginalization and undermine efforts to promote fairness and equality.

9. Social Pressure: Social norms or expectations around respect may create pressure for individuals to conform to certain behaviors or attitudes, even if they do not align with their personal values or beliefs. This can lead to feelings of inauthenticity or dissonance and hinder genuine self-expression.

10. Cultural Misunderstandings: Different cultures may have varying norms or expectations regarding respect, leading to misunderstandings or conflicts when interacting with individuals from diverse backgrounds. Lack of awareness or sensitivity to cultural differences can undermine efforts to build respectful and inclusive relationships.

While respect is generally considered a valuable and important quality, it's essential to be mindful of these potential disadvantages and strive to cultivate respect in ways that are balanced, ethical, and inclusive. By fostering a culture of respect that is grounded in empathy, fairness, and mutual understanding, individuals and communities can work towards building healthier, more harmonious relationships and societies.

Improving respect involves fostering a culture of mutual understanding, empathy, and appreciation for oneself and others. Here are some strategies to enhance respect:

1. Practice Active Listening: Listen attentively to others without interrupting or judging. Show genuine interest in their perspectives and feelings, and validate their experiences by acknowledging their thoughts and emotions.

2. Show Empathy: Put yourself in others' shoes and try to understand their feelings, motivations, and challenges. Demonstrate empathy by expressing compassion, support, and understanding towards their experiences and struggles.

3. Communicate Respectfully: Use polite and considerate language when interacting with others. Avoid disrespectful or derogatory comments, and be mindful of your tone and body language to convey respect and sincerity.

4. Acknowledge Differences: Recognize and appreciate the diversity of perspectives, backgrounds, and experiences among individuals. Embrace cultural, ethnic, and personal differences with an open mind and a willingness to learn from others.

5. Set Boundaries: Establish clear boundaries for yourself and respect the boundaries of others. Communicate your needs, preferences, and limits assertively, and honor the boundaries that others set for themselves.

6. Celebrate Achievements: Acknowledge and celebrate the accomplishments and contributions of others. Show appreciation for their efforts and achievements, and recognize their value and worth as individuals.

7. Offer Constructive Feedback: Provide feedback in a constructive and respectful manner, focusing on specific behaviors or actions rather than personal traits. Offer praise for strengths and opportunities for improvement with empathy and encouragement.

8. Resolve Conflicts Peacefully: Approach conflicts with an open mind and a willingness to find mutually beneficial solutions. Practice active listening, empathy, and compromise to resolve disagreements respectfully and peacefully.

9. Lead by Example: Demonstrate respect in your words and actions, and serve as a role model for others to follow. Treat everyone with kindness,

fairness, and dignity, regardless of their status or background.

10. Promote Inclusivity: Create an inclusive and welcoming environment where everyone feels valued, respected, and included. Foster a culture of diversity and equity by embracing differences and challenging prejudice or discrimination.

11. Educate Yourself: Take the time to educate yourself about different cultures, perspectives, and experiences. Engage in learning opportunities to broaden your understanding of diversity and deepen your empathy towards others.

12. Reflect and Learn: Regularly reflect on your interactions and behaviors to identify areas for improvement. Be open to feedback from others and use it as an opportunity for growth and self-awareness.

By implementing these strategies consistently in your interactions with others, you can contribute to a culture of respect that fosters positive relationships, enhances communication, and promotes empathy and understanding among individuals and communities.

Developing respect involves honing various interpersonal skills that foster empathy, understanding, and consideration for others. Here are some key skills to focus on to cultivate respect:

1. Active Listening: Practice active listening by giving your full attention to others when they speak. Avoid interrupting and show genuine interest in their perspective by asking clarifying questions and summarizing their points.

2. Empathy: Cultivate empathy by putting yourself in others' shoes and trying to understand their feelings, perspectives, and experiences. Practice empathy by acknowledging their emotions and showing compassion and support.

3. Effective Communication: Improve your communication skills by expressing yourself clearly, honestly, and respectfully. Use assertive communication techniques to convey your thoughts and feelings while also respecting the opinions and boundaries of others.

4. Conflict Resolution: Learn conflict resolution skills to address disagreements and conflicts constructively. Practice active listening, empathy, and negotiation to find mutually agreeable solutions and preserve relationships.

5. Self-awareness: Develop self-awareness by reflecting on your own thoughts, feelings, and behaviors. Recognize your biases, triggers, and communication patterns, and strive to manage them effectively in

interactions with others.

6. Respect for Diversity: Foster respect for diversity by embracing differences in culture, ethnicity, gender, religion, and background. Value the unique perspectives and contributions of each individual and treat everyone with dignity and fairness.

7. Boundary Setting: Establish clear boundaries for yourself and respect the boundaries of others. Communicate your needs, preferences, and limits assertively, and honor the boundaries that others set for themselves.

8. Conflict De-escalation: Learn techniques for de-escalating tense situations and managing emotions effectively. Practice calming strategies such as deep breathing, positive self-talk, and taking a break when tensions rise.

9. Patience and Tolerance: Cultivate patience and tolerance by recognizing that everyone has their own pace and perspective. Practice patience in challenging situations and strive to maintain composure and understanding.

10. Continuous Learning: Stay open to learning and growth by seeking out opportunities to expand your knowledge and understanding of different cultures, perspectives, and experiences. Engage in diversity training, cultural competency workshops, and other educational resources to deepen your respect for diversity.

11. Leadership by Example: Lead by example and demonstrate respect in your words and actions. Treat others with kindness, fairness, and dignity, and advocate for a culture of respect and inclusion in your personal and professional spheres.

12. Feedback and Adaptation: Seek feedback from others about your communication style, behavior, and impact on them. Use this feedback as an opportunity for self-reflection and adaptation to improve your interactions and relationships.

By developing these skills and incorporating them into your daily interactions, you can cultivate a deeper sense of respect for others and contribute to a more inclusive, empathetic, and harmonious environment.

Examples of respect can manifest in various ways in different contexts. Here are some examples:

1. Listening attentively: When someone speaks, giving them your full attention, maintaining eye contact, and refraining from interrupting demonstrates respect for their thoughts and opinions.

2. Using inclusive language: Being mindful of the language you use to ensure it is inclusive and respectful of people's identities, backgrounds, and experiences. This includes using preferred pronouns, avoiding stereotypes, and refraining from making assumptions.

3. Acknowledging others' perspectives: Recognizing and valuing the viewpoints of others, even if they differ from your own, shows respect for their autonomy and right to their opinions.

4. Showing appreciation: Expressing gratitude and appreciation for the contributions, efforts, and achievements of others acknowledges their value and demonstrates respect for their contributions.

5. Respecting personal space: Being mindful of people's personal space and boundaries, and refraining from invading it without permission, demonstrates respect for their physical autonomy and comfort.

6. Respecting time: Being punctual and respecting others' time by showing up for meetings and appointments on time, and communicating promptly if you are unable to attend, demonstrates respect for their schedules and commitments.

7. Empathizing with others: Putting yourself in someone else's shoes and showing empathy for their feelings, experiences, and challenges demonstrates respect for their humanity and emotional well-being.

8. Respecting diversity: Embracing and celebrating diversity in all its forms, including race, ethnicity, gender, religion, sexual orientation, and ability, demonstrates respect for the richness of human experience and the dignity of every individual.

9. Respecting authority: Showing deference and obedience to legitimate authority figures, such as teachers, bosses, or public officials, demonstrates respect for their roles and responsibilities.

Resolving conflicts peacefully: Approaching conflicts with a spirit of cooperation and compromise, actively listening to others' perspectives, and seeking mutually beneficial solutions demonstrates respect for the dignity

FOUR
LOVE

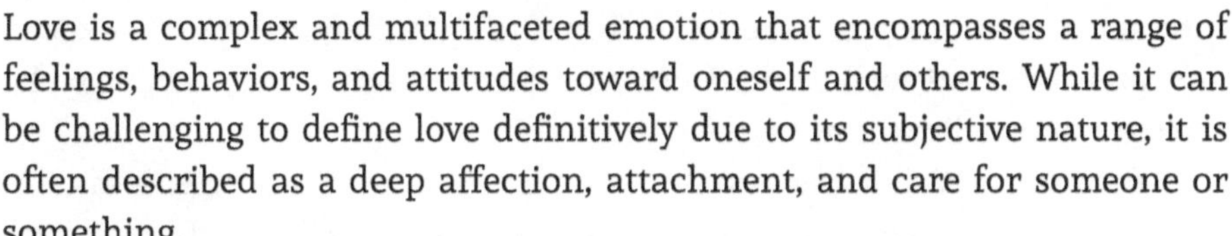

Love is a complex and multifaceted emotion that encompasses a range of feelings, behaviors, and attitudes toward oneself and others. While it can be challenging to define love definitively due to its subjective nature, it is often described as a deep affection, attachment, and care for someone or something.

Here are some key aspects of what love means:

Affection and Fondness: Love involves feelings of warmth, tenderness, and affection toward the object of one's love. It is characterized by a deep emotional connection and a desire to nurture and care for the other person.

Empathy and Understanding: Love involves the ability to empathize with others and understand their thoughts, feelings, and experiences. It requires listening, compassion, and acceptance of the other person's perspectives and emotions.

Respect and Appreciation: Love entails respecting and valuing the unique qualities, strengths, and differences of the person you love. It involves appreciating their individuality, talents, and contributions to your life.

Commitment and Loyalty: Love often involves a commitment to the well-being and happiness of the other person. It includes being loyal, supportive, and dependable, even during challenging times.

Intimacy and Connection: Love fosters a sense of intimacy, closeness, and connection between individuals. It involves sharing thoughts, feelings, and experiences openly and honestly, as well as physical affection and closeness.

Selflessness and Sacrifice: Love may involve acts of selflessness and sacrifice for the well-being and happiness of the other person. It includes putting their needs and interests above your own and making compromises for the sake of the relationship.

Unconditional Acceptance: Love often involves accepting the other person for who they are, flaws and all, without judgment or conditions. It entails embracing their imperfections and loving them unconditionally.

Joy and Fulfillment: Love brings joy, fulfillment, and meaning to life. It provides a sense of purpose, belonging, and connection that enhances overall well-being and happiness.

It's important to recognize that love can take many forms and may be expressed in different ways depending on the nature of the relationship and the individuals involved. Whether it's romantic love, platonic love, familial love, or love for oneself, love enriches our lives and brings depth and meaning to our human experience.

Life without love can feel empty and lacking in fulfillment, as love is a fundamental human need that contributes to our emotional, psychological, and even physical well-being. Here are some aspects of life that may be affected by the absence of love:

1. Emotional Well-being: Love provides us with feelings of happiness, joy, and contentment. Without love, we may experience feelings of loneliness, sadness, and emptiness. Emotional support and connection with others are essential for maintaining a positive outlook on life and coping with stress and challenges.

2. Relationships: Love forms the basis of our relationships with family, friends, and romantic partners. Without love, relationships may feel shallow or strained, and it may be challenging to form meaningful connections with others. Healthy relationships thrive on love, trust, and mutual respect.

3. Self-Esteem: Love plays a significant role in shaping our self-esteem and self-worth. Feeling loved and valued by others helps us develop a positive sense of self and confidence in our abilities. Without love, we may struggle with feelings of inadequacy, self-doubt, and low self-esteem.

4. Purpose and Meaning: Love gives us a sense of purpose and meaning in life. Whether it's caring for loved ones, pursuing passions, or making a difference in the world, love motivates us to live with intention and to strive for fulfillment. Without love, life may feel aimless or meaningless.

5. Physical Health: Love has been linked to better physical health outcomes, including lower blood pressure, reduced stress levels, and improved immune function. Without love, we may be more susceptible to physical ailments and may experience negative health consequences associated with loneliness and social isolation.

6. Creativity and Inspiration: Love has the power to inspire creativity and fuel our passions. Whether it's through art, music, or writing, love often serves as a muse for creative expression. Without love, we may struggle to find inspiration and motivation to pursue our interests and hobbies.

7. Resilience and Coping Skills: Love provides us with a support system during difficult times and helps us develop resilience and coping skills. Without love, we may feel more vulnerable to stress, anxiety, and depression, and may struggle to cope with life's challenges effectively.

While life without love may feel challenging, it's essential to remember that love comes in many forms, and there are opportunities to cultivate love and connection in various aspects of life. Seeking support from friends, family, or a therapist can also help navigate the difficulties of living without love and work towards building fulfilling relationships and a meaningful life.

Love is indeed a vital and intrinsic part of the human experience. Here's why:

1. Emotional Fulfillment: Love brings immense emotional fulfillment and happiness to our lives. Whether it's the love of family, friends, or romantic partners, feeling loved and cherished by others enhances our overall well-being and quality of life.

2. Connection and Belonging: Love fosters a sense of connection, belonging, and intimacy with others. It helps us feel understood, supported, and valued, and strengthens our bonds with the people around us. Love creates a sense of community and shared experiences, which are essential for our social and emotional development.

3. Support and Comfort: Love provides us with a source of support, comfort, and reassurance during difficult times. Knowing that we have someone who cares for us unconditionally gives us the strength and resilience to overcome challenges and navigate life's ups and downs with greater ease.

4. Personal Growth: Love encourages personal growth, self-discovery, and self-improvement. Through our relationships with others, we learn valuable lessons about empathy, compassion, communication, and compromise, which help us become better individuals and cultivate deeper connections with others.

5. Health Benefits: Love has been linked to numerous health benefits, both physical and mental. Studies have shown that people in loving relationships

tend to have lower levels of stress, reduced risk of depression and anxiety, better cardiovascular health, and longer life expectancy. The emotional support and companionship provided by love contribute to overall well-being and longevity.

6. Sense of Purpose: Love gives us a sense of purpose and meaning in life. Whether it's caring for loved ones, nurturing friendships, or pursuing passions and interests, love motivates us to live with intention and to make a positive impact on the world around us. It gives us something to strive for and brings deeper meaning to our existence.

7. Joy and Happiness: Love brings joy, laughter, and happiness into our lives. The simple act of sharing moments of joy with loved ones, whether it's celebrating milestones, creating memories, or enjoying each other's company, fills our hearts with happiness and gratitude for the blessings in our lives.

In summary, love is a fundamental aspect of the human experience that enriches our lives in countless ways. It provides us with emotional fulfillment, strengthens our relationships, promotes personal growth, enhances our well-being, and brings joy and meaning to our lives. Cultivating love and nurturing our relationships with others is essential for living a happy, fulfilling, and meaningful life.

Here are some of the benefits of love:

1. Emotional Well-being: Love can boost our emotional well-being by providing us with feelings of happiness, contentment, and fulfillment. Being in loving relationships can reduce stress, anxiety, and depression while increasing overall life satisfaction.

2. Physical Health: Studies have shown that love can have positive effects on physical health. Being in a loving relationship can lower blood pressure, strengthen the immune system, and reduce the risk of cardiovascular diseases. The emotional support and companionship provided by love can also contribute to faster recovery from illnesses and surgeries.

3. Longevity: People in loving relationships tend to live longer than those who are not. The emotional support and sense of belonging that come with love can promote longevity by reducing the risk of premature death from various causes, including heart disease, stroke, and accidents.

4. Stress Reduction: Love acts as a natural stress reliever. When we feel loved and supported by others, our bodies release hormones like oxytocin and endorphins, which help reduce stress levels. Having someone to share our worries and burdens with can make life's challenges feel more

manageable.

5. Improved Mental Health: Love can have a positive impact on mental health by providing emotional support, validation, and a sense of belonging. Being in loving relationships can lower the risk of developing mental health disorders like depression and anxiety, and it can also help improve self-esteem and self-confidence.

6. Enhanced Resilience: Love can make us more resilient in the face of adversity. Knowing that we have someone who cares for us and supports us unconditionally can give us the strength and courage to overcome life's challenges and bounce back from setbacks more easily.

7. Increased Happiness: Love is closely linked to feelings of happiness and life satisfaction. Whether it's romantic love, familial love, or friendship love, having meaningful connections with others can bring joy and fulfillment to our lives. Sharing experiences, making memories, and feeling valued and appreciated by loved ones can contribute to overall happiness.

8. Sense of Purpose: Love can give us a sense of purpose and meaning in life. Whether it's caring for a partner, raising children, or supporting friends and family, our connections with others give us a reason to strive, grow, and contribute to the world around us.

Overall, love has a multitude of benefits for both our physical and mental well-being. Cultivating loving relationships and connections with others can lead to a happier, healthier, and more fulfilling life.

While love brings many benefits, it's also important to acknowledge that it can come with its own set of challenges and disadvantages:

1. Vulnerability: Love often requires us to open up and make ourselves vulnerable to others. This vulnerability can leave us exposed to hurt and disappointment if the relationship doesn't work out as expected.

2. Heartbreak: One of the most significant disadvantages of love is the potential for heartbreak. When relationships end or when love is not reciprocated, it can cause emotional pain, sadness, and grief.

3. Dependency: Love has the potential to create dependency on others for emotional validation and support. This dependency can lead to feelings of insecurity and a loss of independence if the relationship becomes unhealthy or codependent.

4. Conflict: Love can sometimes lead to conflict and disagreements, particularly in romantic relationships. Differences in opinions, values, and expectations can create tension and strain on the relationship.

5. Jealousy and Possessiveness: Love can sometimes bring out feelings of jealousy and possessiveness, particularly in romantic relationships. These feelings can lead to unhealthy behaviors such as distrust, control, and insecurity.

6. Loss of Identity: In some cases, love can lead to a loss of individual identity as people prioritize the needs and desires of their partner over their own. This can result in a lack of self-fulfillment and personal growth.

7. Social Pressure: Societal expectations and pressures surrounding love and relationships can contribute to feelings of inadequacy or failure if individuals don't meet certain standards or milestones.

8. Risk of Betrayal: Trust is a fundamental component of love, and betrayal can have devastating effects on relationships. Whether it's infidelity, dishonesty, or broken promises, betrayal can erode trust and damage the foundation of love.

9. Loss of Freedom: Love can sometimes lead to a loss of freedom and autonomy, particularly in long-term commitments such as marriage or parenting. Responsibilities and obligations to loved ones can limit individual freedom and flexibility.

10. Emotional Exhaustion: Maintaining healthy relationships requires emotional investment and effort. Love can be emotionally demanding, and constant emotional support and compromise can lead to feelings of exhaustion and burnout over time.

It's important to recognize that while love can bring joy and fulfillment, it also requires effort, communication, and compromise to navigate its challenges and disadvantages effectively.

Youngster love

As a youngster, building romantic relationships and finding love can be an exciting but sometimes challenging journey. Here are some tips to help you navigate the process of finding love as a youngster:

1. Focus on Yourself: Before seeking love from others, focus on developing a strong sense of self-love and self-confidence. Take care of yourself physically, mentally, and emotionally, and engage in activities that bring you joy and fulfillment. When you love and value yourself, others are more likely to be attracted to you.

2. Expand Your Social Circle: Take advantage of opportunities to meet new people and expand your social circle. Join clubs, organizations, or social groups that align with your interests and values. Attend social events, parties, and gatherings where you can meet like-minded individuals and

form new connections.

3. Be Open-Minded: Be open to meeting people from diverse backgrounds and with different interests and perspectives. You never know where you might find love, so keep an open mind and be willing to give people a chance, even if they're not exactly what you expected.

4. Communicate Clearly: When you're interested in someone, communicate your feelings and intentions clearly and respectfully. Strike up conversations, ask questions, and show genuine interest in getting to know them. Be confident, but also be respectful of their boundaries and preferences.

5. Build Friendships First: Focus on building genuine friendships with people you're interested in before pursuing a romantic relationship. Getting to know someone as a friend first can help you establish a strong foundation of trust, compatibility, and mutual respect.

6. Be Yourself: Authenticity is attractive, so be yourself and let your true personality shine through. Don't try to pretend to be someone you're not or conform to someone else's expectations. Embrace your unique qualities and quirks, and be confident in who you are.

7. Take Initiative: If you're interested in someone, don't be afraid to take initiative and make the first move. Ask them out on a date, invite them to hang out, or simply express your feelings and interest in getting to know them better. Remember that rejection is a natural part of the dating process, and it's okay if things don't work out with everyone you're interested in.

8. Be Patient: Finding love takes time, so be patient and don't rush the process. Enjoy the journey of getting to know new people, building connections, and experiencing new adventures along the way. Trust that the right person will come into your life when the time is right.

9. Stay Positive: Stay positive and optimistic, even in the face of rejection or disappointment. Keep an open heart and mind, and trust that love will find its way to you when you least expect it. Focus on the present moment and enjoy the experiences and relationships that come your way.

10. Seek Support: If you're struggling with finding love or navigating relationships, don't hesitate to seek support from friends, family members, or a trusted mentor. They can offer advice, encouragement, and perspective to help you navigate the ups and downs of love and relationships.

Remember that finding love is a journey, and it's okay to take your time and enjoy the process. Keep an open heart, stay true to yourself, and trust that love will find you when the time is right.

Married life love

Maintaining love and nurturing your relationship in married life requires ongoing effort, communication, and commitment from both partners. Here are some tips to help you strengthen the love in your marriage:

1. Prioritize Communication: Open and honest communication is essential for building and maintaining a strong connection with your partner. Take the time to listen actively to each other, express your feelings and needs openly, and discuss any concerns or issues that arise in your relationship.

2. Show Appreciation: Express gratitude and appreciation for your partner regularly. Acknowledge their efforts, strengths, and qualities, and let them know how much you value and love them. Small gestures of appreciation can go a long way in strengthening your bond and deepening your connection.

3. Spend Quality Time Together: Make time for each other in your busy schedules and prioritize spending quality time together. Engage in activities that you both enjoy, whether it's going on dates, taking walks, cooking together, or simply cuddling on the couch. Quality time allows you to connect and strengthen your emotional bond.

4. Keep Romance Alive: Keep the romance alive in your marriage by nurturing intimacy and passion. Plan romantic dates, surprise each other with thoughtful gestures, and prioritize physical affection and intimacy. Keep the spark alive by expressing your love and desire for each other regularly.

5. Support Each Other's Goals: Encourage and support each other in pursuing your individual goals and dreams. Be each other's biggest cheerleaders and celebrate each other's successes. A supportive and nurturing environment fosters love and growth in your relationship.

6. Practice Empathy and Understanding: Seek to understand your partner's perspective and empathize with their feelings and experiences. Validate their emotions, even if you don't always agree, and offer support and comfort during challenging times. Empathy and understanding build trust and strengthen your connection.

7. Resolve Conflicts Constructively: Conflict is a natural part of any relationship, but it's how you handle it that matters. Approach conflicts with a willingness to listen, compromise, and find solutions together. Use "I" statements to express your feelings without blaming or criticizing, and work

towards finding common ground and resolution.

8. Keep the Friendship Alive: Maintain a strong friendship with your partner by enjoying each other's company, sharing laughter and inside jokes, and being each other's confidants. Friendship forms the foundation of a lasting and fulfilling marriage.

9. Practice Forgiveness: Learn to forgive each other for mistakes, misunderstandings, and past hurts. Holding onto grudges and resentment can erode trust and intimacy in your relationship. Choose forgiveness and let go of the past to move forward with love and compassion.

10. Seek Professional Help if Needed: If you're facing challenges in your marriage or struggling to reconnect with your partner, don't hesitate to seek professional help from a couples therapist or counselor. Professional support can provide valuable insights, guidance, and tools to navigate difficult issues and strengthen your relationship.

By prioritizing communication, appreciation, quality time, and mutual support, you can nurture love and deepen your connection with your partner in your married life. Remember that love in marriage requires ongoing effort and commitment from both partners, but the rewards of a strong and loving relationship are immeasurable.

Love as an older adult or senior can be a rewarding and fulfilling experience, regardless of age. Here are some tips to help older adults and seniors navigate the process of finding love:

1. Stay Open-Minded: Be open to the idea of finding love at any age. Love knows no age limits, and meaningful connections can happen at any stage of life. Stay open-minded and optimistic about the possibilities of finding love as an older adult.

2. Expand Your Social Circle: Get involved in activities and communities that interest you and offer opportunities to meet new people. Join clubs, volunteer groups, senior centers, or religious organizations where you can connect with like-minded individuals and form new friendships.

3. Use Online Dating Platforms: Consider using online dating platforms specifically designed for older adults and seniors. These platforms cater to individuals looking for companionship, romance, or friendship later in life and can provide a convenient way to connect with potential partners.

4. Attend Social Events: Attend social events, gatherings, and parties in your community where you can meet new people and socialize. Look for events specifically geared towards older adults or seniors, such as dances, game nights, or cultural outings.

5. Stay Active and Engaged: Stay active physically, mentally, and socially to maintain a vibrant and fulfilling life. Engage in activities that bring you joy, whether it's exercising, pursuing hobbies, or learning new skills. Staying active and engaged can help you meet new people and increase your chances of finding love.

6. Be Authentic: Be authentic and true to yourself when meeting new people. Embrace your unique qualities, experiences, and interests, and don't be afraid to share them with others. Authenticity is attractive and can help you form genuine connections with potential partners.

7. Communicate Clearly: Practice open and honest communication when getting to know someone new. Clearly express your feelings, intentions, and expectations, and listen actively to what the other person has to say. Effective communication is essential for building trust and understanding in a relationship.

8. Take Initiative: Don't be afraid to take initiative and make the first move when you're interested in someone. Ask them out on a date, invite them to join you for an activity, or simply strike up a conversation to get to know them better. Taking initiative shows confidence and can lead to meaningful connections.

9. Be Patient: Finding love takes time, so be patient and don't rush the process. Enjoy getting to know new people, building connections, and exploring potential relationships at your own pace. Trust that the right person will come into your life when the time is right.

10. Seek Support: If you're struggling to find love or feeling discouraged, don't hesitate to seek support from friends, family members, or a therapist. Talking about your feelings and experiences with others can provide perspective, encouragement, and emotional support as you navigate the journey of finding love as an older adult or senior.

Increasing love in relationships involves nurturing and strengthening the emotional connection between individuals. Here are some ways to do so:

1. Communication: Open and honest communication is crucial for building and maintaining love in relationships. Take the time to listen to your partner, express your feelings and needs clearly, and work together to resolve conflicts constructively.

2. Quality Time: Spend quality time together to deepen your bond and connection. This could involve going on dates, engaging in shared hobbies or activities, or simply spending quiet moments together talking and enjoying each other's company.

3. Express Appreciation: Show appreciation and gratitude for your partner regularly. Acknowledge their efforts, strengths, and qualities, and let them know how much they mean to you. Small gestures of appreciation can go a long way in strengthening love.

4. Acts of Kindness: Show kindness and compassion towards your partner by doing thoughtful things for them. Whether it's making them breakfast in bed, sending them a sweet message, or offering a helping hand, acts of kindness can foster love and warmth in the relationship.

5. Physical Affection: Physical touch is a powerful way to express love and affection. Hug, kiss, hold hands, and cuddle with your partner regularly to strengthen your emotional connection and bond.

6. Shared Goals and Dreams: Work together towards shared goals and dreams as a couple. Whether it's traveling the world, buying a house, or starting a family, having common aspirations can create a sense of unity and purpose in the relationship.

7. Trust and Respect: Build a foundation of trust and respect in your relationship by being honest, reliable, and respectful towards your partner. Trust is essential for fostering a deep and lasting connection based on mutual respect and understanding.

8. Celebrate Differences: Embrace and celebrate each other's differences, quirks, and individuality. Respect each other's opinions, perspectives, and boundaries, and appreciate the unique qualities that make you both who you are.

9. Keep Romance Alive: Keep the romance alive in your relationship by surprising each other, being affectionate, and nurturing intimacy. Plan romantic gestures, date nights, and special occasions to keep the spark alive and reignite the passion in your relationship.

10. Work Through Challenges Together: Every relationship faces challenges and obstacles, but it's how you navigate them together that strengthens your love. Approach challenges as a team, support each other through difficult times, and grow stronger together as a result.

By prioritizing communication, connection, and mutual support, you can increase love in your relationship and cultivate a deep and lasting bond with your partner.

Here are some great examples of love from various sources:

1. Romeo and Juliet: This iconic Shakespearean tragedy tells the story of two young lovers from feuding families who defy societal expectations and risk everything for their love.

2. Jane Eyre and Mr. Rochester: In Charlotte Brontë's novel "Jane Eyre," the protagonist Jane finds love and companionship with Mr. Rochester despite their differences in social status and personal struggles.

3. Elizabeth Bennet and Mr. Darcy: Jane Austen's "Pride and Prejudice" features the love story of Elizabeth Bennet and Mr. Darcy, who overcome misunderstandings and societal pressures to find true love and acceptance.

4. Noah and Allie from "The Notebook": This romantic novel by Nicholas Sparks, and its film adaptation, tells the enduring love story of Noah and Allie, who overcome obstacles and stay committed to each other despite the passage of time and the challenges they face.

5. Carl and Ellie from "Up": In the Pixar animated film "Up," the love story of Carl and Ellie is beautifully depicted through a wordless montage that shows their lifelong bond, shared dreams, and unwavering love for each other.

6. Laila and Majnun: This classic Persian tale, also popular in Middle Eastern and South Asian cultures, tells the tragic love story of Laila and Majnun, who are unable to be together due to societal and familial opposition but remain devoted to each other until death.

7. Romeo and Juliet from "West Side Story": Inspired by Shakespeare's tragedy, "West Side Story" portrays the love story of Tony and Maria, two young lovers from rival gangs who face prejudice and violence but are willing to risk everything for their love.

8. Jack and Rose from "Titanic": This epic romance film directed by James Cameron tells the story of Jack and Rose, two passengers aboard the ill-fated RMS Titanic, who fall in love despite the class differences and tragic circumstances surrounding them.

9. Hazel Grace Lancaster and Augustus Waters from "The Fault in Our Stars": In John Green's novel and its film adaptation, Hazel and Augustus, two teenagers battling cancer, find love and solace in each other as they navigate the challenges of illness and mortality.

10. Mufasa and Sarabi from "The Lion King": The relationship between Mufasa and Sarabi in Disney's "The Lion King" exemplifies love, strength, and devotion as they support each other and protect their family in the face of adversity.

11. Radha and Krishna: Radha and Krishna are central figures in Hindu mythology and are revered for their divine love. Their love story, depicted in various scriptures, poetry, and art forms, symbolizes the eternal bond between the devotee and the divine.

12. Shah Jahan and Mumtaz Mahal: Emperor Shah Jahan's love for his wife Mumtaz Mahal is immortalized in the iconic monument, the Taj Mahal. Built as a mausoleum for Mumtaz Mahal, the Taj Mahal is considered one of the most beautiful expressions of love in the world.

13. Heer and Ranjha: The Punjabi folk tale of Heer and Ranjha is a classic love story that transcends social barriers and religious differences. Despite facing opposition from their families, Heer and Ranjha remain devoted to each other until death.

14. Laila and Majnu: The story of Laila and Majnu, originally from Persian literature, has been adapted and celebrated in Indian culture for centuries. Their passionate and tragic love story serves as a symbol of true love and devotion.

15. Ram and Sita: The epic Ramayana portrays the divine love between Lord Rama and his wife Sita. Their love story, filled with trials and tribulations, is revered by millions of Hindus and serves as a guiding light for marital devotion and righteousness.

16. Romeo and Juliet of the East (Mirza Ghalib and Nawab Zeb-un-Nisa): Mirza Ghalib, one of the most celebrated poets in Urdu literature, had a deep and unrequited love for Nawab Zeb-un-Nisa, the daughter of Mughal Emperor Aurangzeb. Their poignant love story is reflected in Ghalib's verses and letters.

These examples showcase the depth, complexity, and enduring power of love across different cultures, time periods, and storytelling mediums.

Cultivate more love in your life or enhance the love in your relationships, there are several remedies and practices you can try:

1. Self-Love: Cultivate a strong sense of self-love and self-worth. Treat yourself with kindness, compassion, and respect. Engage in self-care activities that nourish your body, mind, and soul, such as meditation, journaling, exercise, and spending time in nature.

2. Gratitude Practice: Practice gratitude to cultivate love and appreciation for the blessings in your life. Take time each day to reflect on what you're grateful for and express appreciation for the people you love. Gratitude can help shift your focus from what's lacking to what's abundant in your life.

3. Quality Time: Invest time and effort into building and nurturing meaningful connections with loved ones. Make a conscious effort to spend quality time together, engage in meaningful conversations, and create shared experiences that strengthen your bond and deepen your connection.

4. Acts of Kindness: Show love and kindness to others through small gestures and acts of kindness. Whether it's offering a listening ear, lending a helping hand, or giving compliments, acts of kindness can create positive energy and foster deeper connections with others.

5. Communication: Practice open and honest communication in your relationships. Express your thoughts, feelings, and needs clearly and listen actively to others. Effective communication is essential for understanding, empathy, and resolving conflicts constructively.

6. Forgiveness: Practice forgiveness to let go of past hurts and resentments in your relationships. Holding onto grudges can block the flow of love and create barriers to connection. Choose to forgive others and yourself, and focus on healing and moving forward with an open heart.

7. Mindfulness: Cultivate mindfulness to deepen your awareness and presence in the present moment. Mindfulness practices such as meditation, deep breathing, and mindfulness exercises can help you stay grounded, reduce stress, and cultivate a sense of calm and clarity in your relationships.

8. Express Affection: Show affection and appreciation for your loved ones through words, gestures, and physical touch. Express your love openly and regularly, whether it's saying "I love you," giving hugs and kisses, or writing heartfelt notes.

9. Explore Shared Interests: Discover and explore shared interests and hobbies with your loved ones. Engaging in activities together that you both enjoy can strengthen your bond and create opportunities for fun, laughter, and connection.

10. Seek Professional Support: If you're experiencing challenges in your relationships or struggling to cultivate love in your life, consider seeking support from a therapist, counselor, or relationship coach. Professional support can provide valuable insights, guidance, and tools to navigate challenges and cultivate healthier, more fulfilling relationships.

Remember that cultivating love is an ongoing process that requires effort, intention, and practice. By incorporating these remedies into your life and relationships, you can nurture love, connection, and fulfillment in meaningful ways.

Love is a beautiful and timeless experience that can enrich your life at any age. Stay open to the possibilities, embrace new opportunities, and enjoy the journey of finding love later in life.

FIVE
INTEGRITY

Integrity is the quality of being honest, ethical, and morally upright in all aspects of one's behavior and actions. It involves adhering to strong moral and ethical principles, even when faced with difficult choices or temptations. Someone with integrity demonstrates consistency between their words and actions, acting with sincerity, fairness, and transparency in all their interactions.

Key aspects of integrity include:

1. Honesty: Being truthful and sincere in all communications and dealings, avoiding deception, lies, and deceit.

2. Ethical Behavior: Acting in accordance with moral principles and ethical standards, and upholding a sense of right and wrong in decision-making.

3. Reliability: Demonstrating dependability and trustworthiness by fulfilling commitments, keeping promises, and following through on obligations.

4. Accountability: Taking responsibility for one's actions, acknowledging mistakes, and being willing to face the consequences of one's choices.

5. Consistency: Demonstrating consistency between one's beliefs, values, and actions, and avoiding hypocrisy or double standards.

6. Respect: Treating others with respect, dignity, and fairness, and valuing their rights, opinions, and perspectives.

7. Courage: Having the courage to stand up for what is right, even in the face of adversity, criticism, or peer pressure.

8. Transparency: Being open, truthful, and forthcoming in one's interactions and communications, and avoiding hidden agendas or deceitful behavior.

Overall, integrity is a fundamental quality that underpins trust, respect, and credibility in personal, professional, and societal relationships. It forms the foundation of ethical conduct and contributes to building strong, positive, and mutually beneficial relationships with others.

Integrity is of paramount importance in life for several reasons:

1. Building Trust: Integrity is the cornerstone of trust. When people consistently demonstrate honesty, reliability, and ethical behavior, they earn the trust and respect of others, fostering strong and meaningful relationships in personal and professional settings.

2. Enhancing Reputation: Upholding integrity contributes to a positive reputation and image. Individuals with integrity are perceived as credible, authentic, and trustworthy, leading to increased opportunities for advancement, collaboration, and success.

3. Fostering Respect: Integrity commands respect from others. People who uphold their ethical principles and values, even in challenging circumstances, are admired for their strength of character and moral courage.

4. Supporting Ethical Leadership: Integrity is essential for effective leadership. Leaders who lead with integrity inspire and motivate others through their ethical conduct and moral leadership, fostering a culture of honesty, accountability, and fairness within organizations.

5. Promoting Accountability: Integrity encourages personal responsibility and accountability for one's actions. Individuals who maintain integrity take ownership of their decisions and behavior, acknowledging mistakes and striving to learn and grow from them.

6. Facilitating Communication: Integrity fosters open and honest communication. When people communicate transparently and authentically, based on their principles and values, it builds trust and strengthens relationships with others.

7. Guiding Ethical Decision-Making: Integrity serves as a guide for ethical decision-making. Individuals who prioritize integrity consider the moral implications of their actions and choices, striving to do what is right and honorable, even when it is difficult.

8. Preventing Harm: Integrity helps prevent harm and wrongdoing. When people adhere to ethical standards and values, they avoid actions that could cause harm to themselves or others, contributing to a safer and more just society.

9. Supporting Personal Growth: Cultivating integrity promotes personal growth and development. Individuals who strive to live with integrity continuously reflect on their values, behaviors, and choices, leading to greater self-awareness, resilience, and moral development.

10. Contributing to the Common Good: Ultimately, integrity contributes to the common good and well-being of society. By upholding ethical standards and values, individuals with integrity promote fairness, justice, and the greater good, fostering a culture of trust, respect, and integrity in all aspects of life.

In summary, integrity is essential for fostering trust, respect, and ethical behavior in personal and professional life. It forms the foundation of strong and meaningful relationships, effective leadership, and a just and harmonious society. Cultivating integrity is not only a personal responsibility but also a moral imperative for building a better world for ourselves and future generations.

Integrity is the cornerstone of character and the bedrock upon which trust and respect are built.we delve into the meaning of integrity, its importance in personal and professional life, and how individuals can cultivate and uphold integrity in their actions and decisions.

1.Cultivating Integrity: Integrity is a trait that can be cultivated and strengthened over time through conscious effort and self-reflection. By clarifying personal values, setting high ethical standards, and holding oneself accountable for one's actions, individuals can nurture integrity in themselves and inspire it in others. Cultivating integrity also involves practicing honesty, transparency, and consistency in all interactions and decisions.

2.Challenges to Integrity: Despite its importance, maintaining integrity can be challenging, particularly in situations where ethical dilemmas arise or when faced with external pressures or incentives to compromise one's principles. In this section, we explore common challenges to integrity and strategies for overcoming them, such as seeking guidance from trusted mentors, weighing the consequences of actions, and staying true to one's values.

Integrity is the foundation of character and the cornerstone of ethical conduct. By embodying integrity in our actions and decisions, we not only uphold our personal values and principles but also contribute to a more trustworthy, just, and harmonious world. Through ongoing commitment and vigilance, individuals can cultivate integrity as a guiding principle in their lives, inspiring trust, respect, and admiration from others.

Growing integrity is a lifelong journey that involves cultivating strong moral and ethical principles and consistently aligning one's actions with those principles. Here are some steps to help you developing integrity:

1. Clarify Your Values: Reflect on your core values and principles that guide your behavior and decision-making. Identify what matters most to you, such as honesty, respect, fairness, and compassion. Clarifying your values provides a solid foundation for cultivating integrity.

2. Set High Ethical Standards: Establish high ethical standards for yourself and strive to uphold them in all aspects of your life. Define clear boundaries and guidelines for ethical conduct, and hold yourself accountable for adhering to them, even in challenging situations.

3. Lead by Example: Demonstrate integrity in your actions and decisions, and lead by example for others to follow. Be consistent in your behavior, and strive to be a role model of honesty, fairness, and transparency in your interactions with others.

4. Practice Self-Reflection: Regularly reflect on your thoughts, feelings, and actions to assess whether they align with your values and principles. Be honest with yourself about areas where you may need to improve and commit to continuous self-improvement and growth.

5. Take Responsibility: Take ownership of your actions and decisions, and accept accountability for any mistakes or shortcomings. Avoid making excuses or blaming others for your behavior, and instead focus on learning from your experiences and striving to do better in the future.

6. Seek Feedback: Solicit feedback from trusted friends, mentors, or colleagues about your behavior and actions. Listen with an open mind to their perspectives and insights, and use constructive feedback as an opportunity for self-reflection and growth.

7. Stay True to Your Principles: Stand firm in your convictions and resist the temptation to compromise your principles, even when faced with pressure or incentives to do so. Trust your instincts and uphold your integrity, knowing that doing the right thing is always worth it in the long run.

8. Practice Empathy and Compassion: Cultivate empathy and compassion towards others, and strive to understand their perspectives and experiences. Treat others with kindness, fairness, and respect, and seek to build positive and supportive relationships based on mutual trust and understanding.

9. Learn from Mistakes: Embrace failure and setbacks as opportunities for growth and learning. When you make mistakes or fall short of your ethical standards, acknowledge them, apologize if necessary, and commit to making amends and doing better in the future.

10. Conflict resolution: Learn conflict resolution skills to address disagreements and ethical conflicts constructively and respectfully. Practice active listening, empathy, and negotiation to find mutually acceptable solutions that uphold integrity and preserve relationships.

11. Decision-making: Develop effective decision-making skills to make ethical choices in complex and ambiguous situations. Gather relevant information, consider different perspectives, and weigh the pros and cons of various options before making decisions aligned with your values.

12. Continuous learning: Commit to lifelong learning and personal growth to deepen your understanding of ethics and integrity. Stay informed about ethical issues and trends, seek feedback from others, and actively seek opportunities to develop and refine your integrity skills.

10. Celebrate Successes: Acknowledge and celebrate your successes in demonstrating integrity, no matter how small. Recognize the progress you've made and the positive impact you've had on others through your actions, and use these achievements as motivation to continue growing and strengthening your integrity.

By committing to these steps and incorporating them into your daily life, you can cultivate integrity and become a person of strong moral character and ethical principles. Remember that growing integrity is a lifelong journey, and it requires ongoing effort, self-reflection, and commitment to doing what is right, even when it's difficultTop of Form

Integrity is a fundamental quality that brings numerous benefits to individuals, organizations, and society as a whole. Here are some of the key benefits of integrity:

1. Trustworthiness: Individuals with integrity are perceived as trustworthy and reliable. They consistently demonstrate honesty, fairness, and transparency in their actions and interactions, earning the trust and confidence of others.

2. Credibility: Integrity enhances one's credibility and reputation. People who uphold their ethical principles and values are seen as credible and authentic, leading to increased respect and influence in personal and professional relationships.

3. Strong Relationships: Integrity fosters strong and meaningful relationships based on mutual trust, respect, and transparency. Individuals with integrity build genuine connections with others, fostering loyalty and collaboration in personal and professional settings.

4. Ethical Leadership: Leaders with integrity inspire and motivate others through their ethical conduct and moral leadership. They set a positive example for their team members, fostering a culture of integrity, accountability, and ethical behavior within organizations.

5. Effective Communication: Integrity facilitates open and honest communication, leading to better understanding, collaboration, and problem-solving. Individuals with integrity communicate transparently and authentically, fostering a culture of trust and transparency in relationships and organizations.

6. Positive Reputation: Maintaining integrity contributes to a positive reputation and image, both personally and professionally. People who consistently demonstrate integrity are highly regarded by others, leading to increased opportunities for advancement, collaboration, and success.

7. Peace of Mind: Living with integrity brings peace of mind and a clear conscience. Individuals who uphold their ethical principles and values can navigate life's challenges with confidence and integrity, knowing that they are doing what is right and honorable.

8. Personal Growth: Cultivating integrity promotes personal growth and self-improvement. Individuals who strive to live with integrity continuously reflect on their values, behaviors, and choices, leading to greater self-awareness, resilience, and moral development.

9. Reduced Stress: Integrity reduces stress and anxiety by eliminating the need to deceive, manipulate, or compromise one's values. Individuals who live with integrity experience greater peace of mind and well-being, knowing that they are acting in alignment with their principles.

10. Positive Impact: Ultimately, integrity contributes to a positive impact on individuals, organizations, and society as a whole. By upholding ethical standards and values, individuals with integrity promote fairness, justice, and the common good, fostering a culture of trust, respect, and integrity in all aspects of life.

Integrity brings a multitude of benefits, including trustworthiness, credibility, strong relationships, ethical leadership, effective communication, positive reputation, peace of mind, personal growth, reduced stress, and a positive impact on individuals and society. Cultivating integrity is essential for fostering a culture of trust, respect, and ethical behavior in personal and professional life.

While integrity is generally regarded as a positive attribute, there can be some perceived disadvantages or challenges associated with maintaining integrity in certain situations.

Here are a few potential disadvantages:

1. Vulnerability to Exploitation: Individuals with high levels of integrity may be perceived as more predictable or less likely to engage in unethical behavior, making them potential targets for manipulation or exploitation by others who are willing to bend or break the rules.

2. Personal Sacrifice: Upholding integrity may sometimes require individuals to make personal sacrifices, such as forgoing opportunities for advancement or financial gain when faced with ethical dilemmas that conflict with their values.

3. Conflict with Organizational Culture: In some organizational cultures or environments where unethical behavior is tolerated or even encouraged, individuals who prioritize integrity may face resistance, backlash, or ostracism from colleagues or superiors who do not share their values.

4. Ethical Dilemmas: Maintaining integrity may sometimes lead individuals to confront difficult ethical dilemmas where there are competing interests or values at play. Navigating these dilemmas can be challenging and may require individuals to make tough decisions with potential consequences.

5. Perception of Naivety: Some people may perceive individuals with high levels of integrity as naive or idealistic, especially in competitive or cutthroat environments where unethical behavior is more common. This perception may lead to skepticism or doubt about the individual's ability to succeed.

6. Limited Opportunities: In certain industries or professions where unethical behavior is prevalent or even rewarded, individuals who prioritize integrity may find themselves at a disadvantage when it comes to career advancement or opportunities for growth.

7. Isolation or Alienation: Individuals who uphold integrity in situations where others do not may sometimes feel isolated or alienated from their peers or colleagues who do not share their values. This can lead to feelings of loneliness or frustration.

8. Increased Stress: Upholding integrity in the face of ethical challenges or conflicts may sometimes lead to increased stress or anxiety as individuals wrestle with difficult decisions and strive to do what they believe is right.

9. Potential for Misunderstanding: In some cases, actions taken in the name of integrity may be misunderstood or misinterpreted by others, leading to conflicts or disagreements. Clear communication and transparency are essential to mitigate these risks.

10. Personal Strain: Striving to maintain integrity in all aspects of life can sometimes create personal strain or pressure, particularly when faced with conflicting priorities or demands. Balancing ethical considerations with personal and professional responsibilities can be challenging.

While these potential disadvantages of integrity should be acknowledged, it's important to recognize that the long-term benefits of living with integrity often outweigh any short-term challenges. Integrity forms the foundation of trust, respect, and ethical behavior, and ultimately contributes to personal and professional success and fulfillment.

Here are few examples of Integrity,

A scenario where an employee discovers a mistake in their favor on their paycheck. Despite the temptation to keep the extra money, the employee promptly notifies their supervisor about the error and offers to return the overpayment.

In this example, the employee demonstrates integrity by prioritizing honesty and ethical behavior over personal gain. By taking the honest and principled course of action, the employee upholds their commitment to integrity, even when faced with a difficult decision. This action not only reflects positively on the employee's character but also reinforces trust and credibility within the workplace.

Some more examples of integrity in various contexts:

1. Academic Integrity: A student refrains from cheating on an exam or plagiarizing a paper, choosing instead to do their own work and abide by the academic honesty policies of their institution.

2. Professional Integrity: A lawyer diligently represents their client's interests within the bounds of the law, even if it means advising against pursuing a course of action that may be technically legal but ethically questionable.

3. Business Integrity: A business owner refuses to cut corners or compromise on product quality, prioritizing the satisfaction and safety of their customers over short-term profits.

4. Personal Integrity: A person maintains consistency between their words and actions, keeping promises and commitments even when it may be inconvenient or difficult to do so.

5. Leadership Integrity: A manager takes responsibility for their team's mistakes and failures, admitting when they've made errors in judgment and working to rectify the situation rather than shifting blame onto others.

6. Environmental Integrity: An environmentalist advocates for sustainable practices and conservation efforts, aligning their personal actions with their values by reducing waste, conserving resources, and supporting eco-friendly initiatives.

7. Social Integrity: A community organizer advocates for social justice and equality, working to address systemic issues such as poverty, discrimination, and inequity through peaceful activism and advocacy.

8. Technological Integrity: A software developer prioritizes user privacy and security in their product design, implementing robust data protection measures and transparent user consent mechanisms to safeguard users' information.

9. Medical Integrity: A healthcare provider upholds patient confidentiality and ethical standards of care, prioritizing the well-being and autonomy of their patients while adhering to professional codes of conduct and medical ethics.

10. Legal Integrity: A judge remains impartial and fair in their rulings, basing decisions on the law and evidence rather than personal biases or outside influences, thus upholding the integrity of the judicial system.

These examples illustrate how integrity can manifest across different aspects of life, demonstrating the importance of honesty, ethics, and moral principles in various contexts.

SIX

FREEDOM

Freedom encompasses the state of being free from constraints, limitations, or oppression. It refers to the ability to act, speak, and make choices without undue interference or coercion from external forces. Freedom encompasses various aspects of life, including political, social, economic, and personal freedoms. It allows individuals to pursue their goals, express themselves, and live according to their own beliefs and values. Freedom is often associated with concepts such as autonomy, liberty, and independence, and it is considered a fundamental human right essential for dignity, equality, and justice.

The importance of freedom cannot be overstated, as it is essential for fostering individual well-being, societal progress, and the protection of fundamental human rights. Here are several key reasons why freedom is important:

1. Dignity and Autonomy: Freedom enables individuals to exercise control over their lives, make choices according to their own values and preferences, and pursue their goals with dignity and autonomy.

2. Human Rights: Freedom is a fundamental human right recognized by international law and foundational to the concept of human dignity. It encompasses rights such as freedom of speech, freedom of religion, freedom of assembly, and freedom from discrimination, which are essential for promoting equality, justice, and respect for all individuals.

3. Democratic Governance: Freedom is essential for the functioning of democratic societies, where individuals have the right to participate in political processes, express their opinions, and hold their governments accountable. Without freedom of expression and political participation, democracy cannot thrive.

4. Innovation and Creativity: Freedom fosters an environment conducive to innovation, creativity, and progress. When individuals are free to explore new ideas, challenge existing norms, and take risks without fear of reprisal, it leads to breakthroughs in science, technology, art, and culture.

5. Economic Prosperity: Freedom is closely linked to economic prosperity and development. Free markets, entrepreneurship, and the protection of property rights enable individuals to create wealth, pursue economic opportunities, and improve their standard of living.

6. Social Cohesion: Freedom promotes social cohesion and harmony by allowing individuals from diverse backgrounds to coexist peacefully and respectfully. It encourages tolerance, diversity, and mutual understanding, fostering a sense of community and belonging.

7. Personal Fulfillment: Freedom enables individuals to live authentically and pursue their passions, interests, and aspirations. It provides opportunities for personal growth, self-expression, and fulfillment, leading to greater happiness and well-being.

8. Rule of Law: Freedom is upheld and protected by the rule of law, which ensures that individuals are treated fairly and equally under the law, and that their rights are safeguarded against arbitrary or unjust actions by governments or individuals.

9. Global Peace and Security: Freedom contributes to global peace and security by promoting cooperation, diplomacy, and respect for international norms and agreements. Free societies are less likely to engage in conflict or aggression against one another, fostering stability and security at the international level.

10. Human Flourishing: Ultimately, freedom is essential for human flourishing and the realization of individual and collective potential. It empowers individuals to live meaningful and fulfilling lives, contribute to the common good, and build a better world for future generations.

Freedom is of paramount importance for promoting human dignity, equality, justice, and progress. It is a foundational value that underpins democratic societies, vibrant economies, and thriving communities, and it must be cherished, protected, and defended by individuals, governments, and institutions alike.

Improving freedom in personal life involves empowering oneself to make choices, express opinions, and pursue goals in alignment with one's values and aspirations. Here are some strategies to enhance freedom in personal life:

1. Self-awareness: Reflect on personal values, beliefs, and goals to gain clarity about what truly matters to you. Understanding your priorities and aspirations can guide decision-making and empower you to live authentically.

2. Assertiveness: Develop assertiveness skills to express yourself confidently and assert your rights and boundaries in various situations. Learn to communicate your needs, preferences, and opinions respectfully while respecting the rights of others.

3. Setting Boundaries: Establish healthy boundaries in relationships and interactions to protect your autonomy and well-being. Communicate your boundaries clearly and assertively, and be willing to enforce them when necessary to safeguard your freedom and dignity.

4. Continuous Learning: Cultivate a mindset of lifelong learning and personal growth. Seek out opportunities to expand your knowledge, skills, and experiences, which can broaden your perspective and enhance your capacity to navigate life with greater freedom and confidence.

5. Emotional Intelligence: Develop emotional intelligence skills to understand and manage your emotions effectively. Cultivate self-awareness, self-regulation, empathy, and social skills to navigate interpersonal relationships and conflicts with grace and integrity.

6. Goal Setting: Set clear and achievable goals that align with your values and aspirations. Break down large goals into smaller, actionable steps, and commit to taking consistent action towards their attainment. Goal-setting can provide direction and purpose, empowering you to live a life of meaning and fulfillment.

7. Adaptability: Cultivate adaptability and resilience to navigate life's challenges and uncertainties with grace and flexibility. Embrace change as an opportunity for growth and learning, and develop coping strategies to bounce back from setbacks and adversity.

8. Mindfulness: Practice mindfulness and present-moment awareness to cultivate inner peace and clarity. Tune into your thoughts, feelings, and sensations without judgment, and cultivate a sense of acceptance and gratitude for the present moment.

9. Healthy Lifestyle: Prioritize self-care and well-being by adopting healthy lifestyle habits that nourish your body, mind, and spirit. Get regular exercise, eat nutritious foods, prioritize sleep, and engage in activities that bring you joy and fulfillment.

10. Seeking Support: Don't hesitate to seek support from trusted friends, family members, or professionals when needed. Surround yourself with people who respect and support your freedom to be yourself and pursue your goals, and offer the same support to others in return.

11. Protect Civil Liberties: Ensure that laws and policies protect fundamental civil liberties, such as freedom of speech, freedom of assembly, freedom of the press, and freedom of religion. Uphold the rights of individuals to express themselves, peacefully protest, and participate in civic life without fear of persecution or censorship.

12. Promote Political Participation: Encourage political participation and engagement among citizens by facilitating voter registration, providing access to unbiased information, and promoting civic education. Empower individuals to actively participate in elections, advocate for policy changes, and hold their representatives accountable.

13. Strengthen Rule of Law: Uphold the rule of law by ensuring that legal frameworks are transparent, fair, and applied equally to all individuals. Strengthen independent judiciaries, law enforcement agencies, and regulatory bodies to safeguard against corruption, abuse of power, and arbitrary actions by authorities.

14. Combat Discrimination and Inequality: Address systemic discrimination and inequality based on factors such as race, gender, ethnicity, religion, sexual orientation, disability, or socioeconomic status. Promote policies and initiatives that foster inclusivity, diversity, and equal opportunities for all members of society.

15. Protect Human Rights: Uphold and protect human rights as enshrined in international agreements and treaties. Combat human rights abuses, including torture, arbitrary detention, forced labor, and discrimination, through legal mechanisms, advocacy efforts, and international cooperation.

16. Support Freedom of the Press: Defend freedom of the press and ensure that journalists can report on matters of public interest without censorship, harassment, or intimidation. Protect journalists' safety and independence, and promote media literacy to counter disinformation and propaganda.

17. Promote Economic Freedom: Foster economic freedom by reducing barriers to entrepreneurship, trade, and investment. Create a conducive environment for business growth, innovation, and job creation, while ensuring social safety nets and protections for workers.

18. Invest in Education: Invest in quality education that empowers individuals with critical thinking skills, knowledge, and information literacy. Promote education initiatives that foster respect for diversity, tolerance, and democratic values from an early age.

19. Encourage Dialogue and Debate: Create spaces for open dialogue, debate, and deliberation on social, political, and economic issues. Encourage respectful exchange of ideas, diverse perspectives, and constructive criticism to promote understanding and collaboration.

20. Lead by Example: Lead by example by upholding democratic principles, respecting human rights, and promoting freedom both domestically and internationally. Set a positive example for other countries and inspire global cooperation in advancing freedom and democracy.

By implementing these strategies, you can cultivate a sense of freedom and empowerment in your personal life, allowing you to live authentically, pursue your passions, and thrive in all areas of your life.Societies can work towards improving freedom and creating a more just, inclusive, and prosperous world for all individuals.

Freedom brings numerous benefits to individuals, societies, and nations, fostering well-being, progress, and prosperity. Here are some key benefits of freedom:

1. Individual Autonomy: Freedom empowers individuals to make choices and decisions about their lives, allowing them to pursue their interests, aspirations, and values without undue interference or coercion from external forces.

2. Personal Growth: Freedom creates opportunities for personal growth, self-discovery, and fulfillment. Individuals can explore their potential, develop new skills, and overcome challenges, leading to greater resilience and confidence.

3. Innovation and Creativity: Freedom fosters an environment conducive to innovation, creativity, and entrepreneurship. When individuals are free to explore new ideas, challenge existing norms, and take risks, it leads to breakthroughs in science, technology, art, and culture.

4. Economic Prosperity: Freedom is closely linked to economic prosperity and development. Free markets, entrepreneurship, and the protection of property rights enable individuals to create wealth, pursue economic opportunities, and improve their standard of living.

5. Social Cohesion: Freedom promotes social cohesion and harmony by allowing individuals from diverse backgrounds to coexist peacefully and

respectfully. It encourages tolerance, diversity, and mutual understanding, fostering a sense of community and belonging.

6. Democratic Governance: Freedom is essential for the functioning of democratic societies, where individuals have the right to participate in political processes, express their opinions, and hold their governments accountable. It ensures that governments are responsive to the needs and aspirations of their citizens.

7. Human Rights: Freedom encompasses fundamental human rights such as freedom of speech, freedom of religion, freedom of assembly, and freedom from discrimination. Upholding these rights promotes equality, justice, and respect for all individuals.

8. Quality of Life: Freedom contributes to a higher quality of life by providing individuals with opportunities for education, healthcare, and social mobility. It enhances well-being, happiness, and life satisfaction, leading to healthier and more resilient communities.

9. Global Peace and Security: Freedom contributes to global peace and security by promoting cooperation, diplomacy, and respect for international norms and agreements. Free societies are less likely to engage in conflict or aggression against one another, fostering stability and security at the international level.

10. Human Flourishing: Ultimately, freedom is essential for human flourishing and the realization of individual and collective potential. It empowers individuals to live meaningful and fulfilling lives, contribute to the common good, and build a better world for future generations.

Freedom brings numerous benefits to individuals, societies, and nations, promoting well-being, progress, and prosperity across all aspects of life. It is a foundational value that underpins democratic societies, vibrant economies, and thriving communities, and it must be cherished, protected, and defended by individuals, governments, and institutions alike.

While freedom brings numerous benefits, it can also present some challenges and disadvantages in certain contexts. Here are some potential drawbacks of freedom:

1. Responsibility Overload: With freedom comes responsibility. Individuals may feel overwhelmed by the burden of making decisions and taking accountability for their actions, especially when faced with complex choices or consequences.

2. Existential Anxiety: Too much freedom can lead to existential anxiety as individuals grapple with the uncertainty and ambiguity of life. The

freedom to choose one's path can evoke feelings of fear, doubt, and existential angst about the meaning and purpose of life.

3. Risk of Failure: Freedom allows individuals to pursue their goals and aspirations, but it also exposes them to the risk of failure. Fear of failure or making the wrong choices can paralyze individuals and prevent them from fully embracing their freedom to explore new opportunities.

4. Social Isolation: Exercising freedom may lead to social isolation if individuals prioritize their autonomy over social connections. The pursuit of personal interests and goals may result in alienation from friends, family, or community, leading to feelings of loneliness or disconnection.

5. Conflict with Authority: Asserting one's freedom may lead to conflict with authority figures or institutions that seek to impose rules or restrictions. Individuals may face backlash or punishment for challenging the status quo or exercising their rights in ways that are perceived as disruptive or threatening.

6. Loss of Structure: Freedom can disrupt the sense of structure and routine that provides stability and predictability in life. Without external constraints or guidance, individuals may struggle to establish a sense of order and discipline in their daily lives, leading to chaos or aimlessness.

7. Lack of Direction: Unlimited freedom can be overwhelming for individuals who lack clear goals or direction in life. Without external constraints or guidance, they may struggle to find purpose and meaning, drifting from one pursuit to another without a sense of fulfillment.

8. Vulnerability to Exploitation: Excessive freedom can make individuals vulnerable to exploitation by others who seek to manipulate or take advantage of their autonomy. Without safeguards or protections in place, individuals may fall prey to scams, coercion, or abuse of their trust.

9. Loss of Identity: The pursuit of freedom may lead individuals to question their identity and values as they navigate the complexities of choice and self-expression. Freedom can challenge preconceived notions of identity, forcing individuals to confront uncertainty about who they are and what they stand for.

10. Misuse of Liberties: Excessive freedom may lead to the misuse or abuse of liberties, such as freedom of speech, resulting in hate speech, misinformation, or incitement to violence. Individuals may exploit their freedoms to harm others or undermine societal values.

11. Social Fragmentation: Too much freedom can lead to social fragmentation and polarization, as individuals retreat into echo chambers

or pursue narrow self-interests without regard for the common good. This can weaken social cohesion and undermine efforts to address collective challenges.

12. Inequality: Freedom can exacerbate inequality when certain individuals or groups have greater access to resources, opportunities, or rights than others. Economic freedoms, for example, may widen the gap between the rich and poor, leading to social unrest and resentment.

13. Anarchy and Lawlessness: Absolute freedom without proper regulation or governance can result in anarchy and lawlessness. In the absence of rules and enforcement mechanisms, individuals may engage in criminal behavior or exploit others without consequences, leading to chaos and insecurity.

14. Exploitation and Abuse: Freedoms can be exploited by powerful individuals or entities to exploit and abuse vulnerable populations. For example, economic freedom may lead to exploitation of workers or environmental degradation in pursuit of profit.

15. Social Pressure and Conformity: In societies with high levels of freedom, individuals may face social pressure to conform to certain norms or expectations, limiting their ability to express dissenting opinions or pursue alternative lifestyles without fear of judgment or ostracism.

16. Loss of Social Cohesion: Excessive individual freedoms may erode social cohesion and collective identity, leading to a breakdown of community bonds and mutual trust. This can result in feelings of isolation, alienation, and disconnection from others.

17. Undermining Authority: Excessive freedom may undermine legitimate authority and institutions, leading to a breakdown of governance and social order. Without respect for authority and the rule of law, societies may struggle to maintain stability and address common challenges.

18. External Threats: Freedom can make societies vulnerable to external threats, such as terrorism or foreign interference, if not accompanied by strong defense mechanisms and cooperation with other nations.

19. Lack of Accountability: In societies with high levels of freedom, individuals or groups may evade accountability for their actions, leading to impunity and a culture of lawlessness. This can undermine trust in institutions and the rule of law.

Overall, while freedom is essential for promoting individual autonomy, self-expression, and personal growth, it also poses challenges and risks that individuals must navigate in order to realize its full potential. Finding a balance between freedom and responsibility is key to overcoming the disadvantages and harnessing the benefits of freedom in individual life.Freedom is essential for promoting individual autonomy, human rights, and societal progress, it must be balanced with responsibility, accountability, and respect for the well-being of others and the common good.

Freedom in personal life can manifest in various ways, reflecting an individual's ability to make choices and live according to their values and preferences. Here are some examples:

1.Career Choice: Having the freedom to choose a career path that aligns with your passions and interests, rather than being forced into a job due to external pressures or economic necessity.

2.Living Arrangements: The ability to decide where you live, whether it's in a particular city, country, or type of housing, based on your personal preferences and lifestyle.

3.Relationships: Freedom to choose whom you associate with, including friends and romantic partners, and the ability to leave relationships that are unhealthy or unfulfilling.

4.Expression: The right to express your opinions, beliefs, and emotions openly without fear of repression or discrimination.

5.Education: Access to educational opportunities and the ability to choose what and where you study, empowering you to pursue your intellectual and professional goals.

6.Health and Wellness: Having control over your health decisions, such as choosing your healthcare providers, making informed choices about medical treatments, and adopting a lifestyle that promotes physical and mental well-being.

7.Hobbies and Interests: The liberty to pursue hobbies and interests that bring you joy and satisfaction, from sports and arts to travel and learning new skills.

8.Spirituality: Freedom to practice a religion or spiritual belief system of your choice, or to choose not to follow any religious or spiritual path.

9.Financial Independence: The ability to manage your finances, make decisions about spending and saving, and work towards financial goals that ensure your security and autonomy.

10.Time Management: The flexibility to allocate your time according to your priorities, whether it's balancing work and leisure, spending time with loved ones, or engaging in personal growth activities.

These examples highlight how freedom in personal life is integral to overall well-being and fulfillment, allowing individuals to live authentically and pursue their unique paths.

1. Nelson Mandela: Mandela, the former President of South Africa, is a symbol of freedom and resilience. He spent 27 years in prison for his anti-apartheid activism before eventually leading his country to democracy and becoming its first black president. Mandela's unwavering commitment to justice and equality exemplifies the power of freedom to overcome oppression and achieve positive change.

2. Rosa Parks: Parks, often referred to as the "mother of the civil rights movement," famously refused to give up her seat to a white passenger on a segregated bus in Montgomery, Alabama, in 1955. Her act of defiance sparked the Montgomery Bus Boycott and became a symbol of the struggle for racial equality and freedom.

3. Malala Yousafzai: Yousafzai, a Pakistani education activist, survived an assassination attempt by the Taliban at the age of 15 for her advocacy of girls' education. Despite facing grave danger, she continued to speak out for the rights of girls and women, becoming the youngest-ever Nobel Prize laureate. Yousafzai's courage and determination illustrate the transformative power of freedom to fight for justice and equality.

4. Harriet Tubman: Tubman, an African American abolitionist and political activist, escaped from slavery in the early 19th century and went on to become a leading figure in the Underground Railroad, a network of safe houses and routes used by enslaved people to escape to free states and Canada. Tubman's courageous actions saved hundreds of enslaved individuals and epitomized the pursuit of freedom against incredible odds.

5. The Fall of the Berlin Wall: The dismantling of the Berlin Wall in 1989 symbolized the end of communist rule in Eastern Europe and the reunification of Germany. The event marked a triumph of freedom over oppression and division, allowing people on both sides of the wall to reunite with loved ones, travel freely, and embrace newfound political and economic freedoms.

6. The Arab Spring: The Arab Spring, a series of pro-democracy protests and uprisings that swept across the Middle East and North Africa in 2010-2011, demonstrated the desire of millions of people for freedom, democracy, and human rights. Despite facing repression and violence from authoritarian regimes, protesters bravely took to the streets to demand political reform and greater freedoms.

7. The Civil Rights Movement: The Civil Rights Movement in the United States, led by figures such as Martin Luther King Jr., aimed to end racial segregation and discrimination against African Americans. Through nonviolent protests, boycotts, and acts of civil disobedience, activists challenged unjust laws and policies, ultimately leading to landmark legislation such as the Civil Rights Act of 1964 and the Voting Rights Act of 1965.

These examples showcase the transformative power of freedom to inspire change, challenge injustice, and create a more just, equal, and inclusive world for all individuals.

SEVEN
PEACE

Peace is a state of harmony characterized by the absence of conflict, violence, or disturbance. It encompasses tranquility, serenity, and mutual respect among individuals, communities, and nations. Peace can exist at various levels, including inner peace within oneself, social peace within communities, and global peace among nations. It involves fostering understanding, cooperation, and empathy, as well as resolving disputes and addressing underlying causes of conflict. Ultimately, peace is essential for promoting human well-being, dignity, and prosperity, and for building a more just, equitable, and sustainable world.

Peace refers to a state of harmony, tranquility, and absence of conflict or violence. It encompasses inner calmness, mutual respect, and cooperation among individuals, communities, and nations. Here are some aspects and importance of peace:

Peace in personal life is fundamental for numerous reasons, impacting both mental and physical well-being, as well as overall quality of life. Here are some key points highlighting its importance:

1.Mental Health

Reduces Stress: Peaceful living helps lower stress levels, which can prevent anxiety and depression.

Improves Focus and Clarity: A calm mind is better able to concentrate, make decisions, and solve problems effectively.

Enhances Emotional Regulation: Peace fosters emotional stability, allowing individuals to respond to situations thoughtfully rather than react impulsively.

2.Physical Health

Boosts Immune System: Reduced stress from a peaceful life can enhance the immune system's functionality.

Lowers Risk of Chronic Diseases: Peaceful living can decrease the risk of conditions like hypertension, heart disease, and diabetes.

Improves Sleep: A tranquil mind leads to better sleep quality, which is essential for overall health.

3.Relationships

Promotes Healthy Relationships: Peaceful individuals are more likely to build and maintain positive relationships, fostering mutual respect and understanding.

Reduces Conflict: Inner peace helps in managing conflicts constructively, leading to more harmonious interactions.

4.Productivity and Creativity

Enhances Productivity: A peaceful state of mind increases efficiency and effectiveness in completing tasks.

Stimulates Creativity: A calm and peaceful environment can inspire creative thinking and innovation.

5.Personal Growth

Facilitates Self-Reflection: Peaceful moments allow for introspection, helping individuals understand themselves better and grow personally.

Encourages Mindfulness: Peaceful living promotes mindfulness, which can lead to greater appreciation of the present moment and overall contentment.

6.Overall Quality of Life

Increases Happiness: Peace is closely linked to happiness and life satisfaction.

Promotes Balance: A peaceful life helps in balancing various aspects of life, such as work, relationships, and personal time.

7. Inner Peace: Inner peace is a state of mental and emotional well-being characterized by feelings of serenity, contentment, and harmony. It involves cultivating a sense of mindfulness, acceptance, and gratitude, and finding balance amidst life's challenges and uncertainties.

8. Social Peace: Social peace refers to the absence of conflict, violence, and injustice within communities and societies. It involves fostering equality, tolerance, and respect for diversity, and promoting social cohesion and inclusion among different groups and individuals.

9. Global Peace: Global peace refers to the absence of war, conflict, and hostility among nations and regions. It involves promoting diplomacy,

dialogue, and cooperation to resolve disputes and address shared challenges such as poverty, climate change, and human rights violations.

10. Human Rights: Peace is closely linked to the protection and promotion of human rights, including the right to life, liberty, and security of person. Upholding human rights principles such as equality, justice, and dignity is essential for building peaceful and inclusive societies.

11. Environmental Peace: Environmental peace emphasizes the importance of preserving and protecting the natural environment to ensure the well-being of present and future generations. Addressing environmental degradation, climate change, and biodiversity loss is crucial for promoting peace and sustainability.

12. Conflict Resolution: Peace involves the peaceful resolution of conflicts through dialogue, negotiation, and mediation, rather than resorting to violence or coercion. Building trust, understanding, and empathy among conflicting parties is essential for achieving lasting peace and reconciliation.

13. Economic Stability: Peace is conducive to economic stability and prosperity, as it creates a conducive environment for investment, trade, and development. By reducing the risks of conflict and instability, peace enables individuals and communities to thrive economically and improve their quality of life.

14. Health and Well-being: Peace contributes to the health and well-being of individuals and communities by reducing stress, trauma, and insecurity associated with conflict and violence. Access to healthcare, education, and social services is essential for promoting peace and resilience.

15. Cultural Harmony: Peace involves respecting and celebrating cultural diversity while fostering dialogue and understanding among different cultural, religious, and ethnic groups. Promoting cultural exchange, tolerance, and mutual respect helps build bridges and strengthen social cohesion.

16. Spiritual Fulfillment: Peace is often associated with spiritual fulfillment and a sense of interconnectedness with oneself, others, and the world. Practices such as meditation, prayer, and mindfulness can cultivate inner peace and a deeper sense of purpose and meaning in life.

Peace is a fundamental human aspiration and a prerequisite for realizing the full potential of individuals, communities, and societies. It requires collective effort, commitment, and collaboration at all levels to build a more peaceful and sustainable world for future generations.

Peace offers numerous personal benefits that contribute to overall well-being and quality of life. Here are some of the key personal benefits of experiencing peace:

1. Emotional Well-being: Peace fosters a sense of calmness, tranquility, and emotional stability. It helps individuals manage stress, anxiety, and negative emotions more effectively, leading to greater emotional resilience and well-being.

2. Improved Mental Health: Experiencing peace can have positive effects on mental health by reducing symptoms of depression, anxiety, and other mental health disorders. It allows individuals to cultivate a more positive mindset, cope with challenges, and maintain mental clarity and focus.

3. Enhanced Relationships: Peaceful individuals tend to have healthier and more fulfilling relationships with others. They are better able to communicate effectively, resolve conflicts constructively, and cultivate empathy, trust, and mutual respect in their interactions with friends, family, and colleagues.

4. Better Physical Health: Peace has been associated with improved physical health outcomes, including lower blood pressure, reduced risk of cardiovascular disease, and enhanced immune function. By reducing stress and promoting relaxation, peace supports overall physical well-being and longevity.

5. Increased Productivity: Peaceful individuals often experience higher levels of productivity and efficiency in their personal and professional lives. They are better able to focus their attention, make sound decisions, and achieve their goals with greater clarity and purpose.

6. Greater Resilience: Peace fosters resilience by equipping individuals with the inner strength and coping mechanisms to navigate life's challenges and setbacks. Peaceful individuals are better able to adapt to change, bounce back from adversity, and maintain a sense of perspective and optimism in the face of difficulties.

7. Improved Sleep Quality: Peaceful states of mind promote better sleep quality and overall sleep hygiene. Individuals who experience peace are more likely to enjoy restful, rejuvenating sleep, which is essential for physical, mental, and emotional health.

8. Enhanced Creativity: Peaceful environments stimulate creativity and innovation by providing space for reflection, inspiration, and exploration of new ideas. Peaceful individuals are more open to creative insights and solutions, leading to greater personal and professional growth.

9. Increased Happiness: Ultimately, peace contributes to a greater sense of happiness, fulfillment, and life satisfaction. By fostering inner contentment, harmony, and purpose, peace allows individuals to experience greater joy and meaning in their lives.

Overall, experiencing peace has profound personal benefits that contribute to holistic well-being and a higher quality of life. Cultivating peace in one's life through mindfulness, self-care, and healthy coping strategies can lead to greater resilience, happiness, and fulfillment.

While peace is generally considered desirable and beneficial, there can be certain disadvantages or challenges associated with it, especially in certain contexts. Here are some potential drawbacks of peace:

1. Complacency: In times of peace, there may be a tendency for individuals or societies to become complacent and less vigilant about potential threats or risks. This can lead to a lack of preparedness for unexpected challenges or conflicts that may arise.

2. Stagnation: Without the impetus of conflict or adversity, there may be less motivation for innovation, progress, or improvement. In some cases, prolonged periods of peace can result in stagnation or a lack of growth in various areas of life, including social, economic, or cultural development.

3. Undermining Vigilance: Peace may lead to a reduction in vigilance or security measures, as individuals or authorities perceive fewer immediate threats. However, this can create vulnerabilities and opportunities for exploitation by malicious actors or disruptive forces.

4. Social Inequality: While peace is generally conducive to social stability, it may also perpetuate or exacerbate existing inequalities within society. In the absence of conflict, issues such as poverty, discrimination, and injustice may receive less attention or urgency, leading to social stagnation or marginalization of certain groups.

5. Loss of Preparedness: Prolonged periods of peace can erode the readiness or capacity of individuals, organizations, or governments to respond effectively to potential crises or emergencies. Without regular training or exercises, skills may deteriorate, and response mechanisms may become less effective.

6. Economic Disruption: Sudden transitions from conflict to peace can sometimes disrupt economic systems or industries that have become dependent on conflict-related activities, such as defense spending or arms production. Adjusting to a peace economy may require significant restructuring and adaptation.

7. Cultural Erosion: In some cases, peace can lead to the erosion of cultural traditions, values, or identities that were previously upheld or reinforced through conflict or adversity. Rapid modernization or globalization may accelerate this process, resulting in the loss of cultural diversity or heritage.

8. Political Instability: While peace is generally associated with political stability, abrupt transitions from conflict to peace can sometimes create power vacuums or destabilize existing political structures. This can lead to uncertainty, factionalism, or struggles for power, potentially undermining the peace process.

9. Loss of Unity: In situations where peace is achieved through compromise or negotiation, there may be lingering divisions or resentments among conflicting parties. Maintaining peace may require ongoing efforts to address underlying grievances and build trust and reconciliation.

10. Psychological Challenges: For individuals who have experienced trauma or hardship during times of conflict, transitioning to peace may present psychological challenges such as post-traumatic stress disorder (PTSD) or feelings of disorientation or loss. Healing and rebuilding trust may take time and effort.

It's important to recognize that while peace is generally preferable to conflict, it also comes with its own set of complexities and challenges. Addressing these potential disadvantages requires careful planning, proactive measures, and ongoing commitment to building and sustaining peace in all its dimensions.

Improving peace requires efforts at individual, community, national, and global levels. Here are some ways to contribute to peace-building:

1.Mindfulness and Meditation

Practice Mindfulness: Engage in mindfulness techniques, such as deep breathing, progressive muscle relaxation, or mindful walking, to stay present and reduce stress.

Meditation: Regular meditation can help calm the mind, reduce anxiety, and improve overall mental clarity.

Physical Health

Exercise Regularly: Physical activity releases endorphins, which can improve mood and reduce stress.

Healthy Diet: Eating nutritious food can positively impact your physical and mental well-being.

Adequate Sleep: Ensure you get sufficient, quality sleep to help your body and mind rejuvenate.

2.Time Management

Prioritize Tasks: Organize your day by prioritizing tasks, focusing on what's important, and breaking down larger tasks into manageable steps.

Set Boundaries: Learn to say no when necessary to avoid overcommitting and spreading yourself too thin.

3.Emotional Well-being

Practice Gratitude: Keep a gratitude journal to regularly remind yourself of the positive aspects of your life.

Seek Support: Talk to friends, family, or a therapist when you need emotional support or guidance.

4.Environment

Create a Peaceful Space: Design a tranquil environment at home, with elements that promote relaxation, such as soft lighting, calming colors, and minimal clutter.

Spend Time in Nature: Regularly spend time outdoors to connect with nature, which can be incredibly grounding and stress-relieving.

5.Personal Growth

Engage in Hobbies: Pursue activities that you enjoy and that bring you a sense of fulfillment and joy.

Continuous Learning: Engage in activities that stimulate your mind, such as reading, learning new skills, or taking up new challenges.

6.Relationship Management

Communicate Effectively: Practice open and honest communication in your relationships to foster understanding and reduce conflicts.

Develop Empathy: Cultivate empathy to better understand and connect with others, promoting harmonious relationships.

7.Spiritual Practices

Reflective Practices: Engage in reflective activities such as journaling, prayer, or meditation to connect with your inner self and find meaning.

Community Engagement: Participate in community activities or groups that align with your values and beliefs to create a sense of belonging.

8.Stress Management

Relaxation Techniques: Learn and regularly practice relaxation techniques such as yoga, tai chi, or deep breathing exercises.

Manage Triggers: Identify and manage stress triggers in your life, developing strategies to cope with or eliminate them.

9. Promoting Understanding and Dialogue: Foster empathy, respect, and understanding among individuals and communities by engaging in open and constructive dialogue. Listen to diverse perspectives, seek common ground, and address misunderstandings or grievances through peaceful communication.

10. Advocating for Human Rights: Support and advocate for the protection of human rights, equality, and justice for all individuals, regardless of race, religion, gender, or ethnicity. Speak out against discrimination, oppression, and injustice, and work towards creating inclusive and equitable societies.

11. Resolving Conflicts Peacefully: Seek non-violent and constructive ways to resolve conflicts and disputes, whether at the interpersonal, community, or international levels. Utilize mediation, negotiation, and conflict resolution techniques to address underlying issues and build sustainable peace.

12. Promoting Education and Empowerment: Invest in education, literacy, and skill development to empower individuals and communities to overcome poverty, inequality, and social exclusion. Education fosters critical thinking, tolerance, and understanding, laying the foundation for peaceful coexistence and social cohesion.

13. Supporting Sustainable Development: Address the root causes of conflict and instability by promoting sustainable development, economic opportunity, and environmental stewardship. Invest in infrastructure, healthcare, and social services to improve livelihoods and reduce disparities, contributing to long-term peace and stability.

14. Building Social Cohesion: Foster social cohesion and solidarity by promoting inclusive policies, social integration, and community participation. Support initiatives that bring people together across lines of difference, celebrate diversity, and strengthen social bonds.

15. Empowering Women and Youth: Recognize the important roles of women and youth in peace-building efforts and empower them to participate in decision-making processes and community initiatives. Invest in education, leadership development, and economic opportunities for women and youth to contribute to peace and development.

16. Promoting Good Governance: Advocate for accountable, transparent, and inclusive governance structures that respect the rule of law, uphold human rights, and promote democratic principles. Combat corruption, impunity, and abuse of power to build trust and confidence in public

institutions.

17. Addressing Root Causes of Conflict: Address underlying drivers of conflict such as poverty, inequality, marginalization, and lack of access to resources. Support initiatives that address economic disparities, promote social justice, and address grievances through inclusive and participatory processes.

18. Building Global Solidarity: Recognize that peace is a global responsibility and collaborate with international partners, organizations, and civil society actors to address shared challenges and promote peace and security worldwide. Support multilateral diplomacy, cooperation, and peacekeeping efforts to resolve conflicts and prevent violence.

By collectively embracing these principles and taking concrete actions at all levels of personallife, society, we can contribute to building a more peaceful, just, and sustainable world for present and future generations.

Here are some great examples of individuals, movements, and initiatives that have contributed to promoting peace:

1. Mahatma Gandhi: Mahatma Gandhi, known for his philosophy of nonviolence and civil disobedience, led India to independence from British rule through peaceful resistance. His teachings and actions inspired countless individuals and movements around the world, advocating for social justice, equality, and peace.

2. Nelson Mandela: Nelson Mandela, South Africa's first black president, played a pivotal role in ending apartheid and promoting reconciliation and peace in the country. Despite spending 27 years in prison, Mandela emerged as a symbol of forgiveness, unity, and democracy, fostering peace and reconciliation among South Africa's diverse communities.

3. Martin Luther King Jr.: Martin Luther King Jr., a prominent leader of the American civil rights movement, advocated for nonviolent protest and racial equality. His leadership and activism led to significant legislative and social reforms, advancing the cause of civil rights and promoting peace and justice in the United States.

4. Mother Teresa: Mother Teresa, a Nobel Peace Prize laureate, dedicated her life to serving the poor, sick, and marginalized in society. Through her humanitarian work and compassion, she inspired countless individuals to embrace love, kindness, and peace in their communities.

5. Malala Yousafzai: Malala Yousafzai, a Pakistani activist for female education and the youngest Nobel Prize laureate, bravely spoke out against the Taliban's efforts to deny girls' education in Pakistan. Despite facing

violence and persecution, Malala continues to advocate for education, gender equality, and peace worldwide.

6. The Dalai Lama: The Dalai Lama, spiritual leader of Tibetan Buddhism, advocates for peace, compassion, and interfaith dialogue. Through his teachings and advocacy, he promotes understanding, harmony, and nonviolence as paths to achieving global peace and happiness.

7. United Nations: The United Nations (UN) plays a central role in promoting peace, security, and development worldwide. Through its peacekeeping missions, humanitarian assistance, and diplomatic efforts, the UN seeks to prevent conflict, protect human rights, and promote international cooperation and dialogue.

8. International Peace Day: International Peace Day, observed annually on September 21st, provides an opportunity for individuals and communities worldwide to come together in the spirit of peace and nonviolence. It serves as a reminder of the importance of promoting tolerance, understanding, and cooperation to build a more peaceful world.

9. The Good Friday Agreement: The Good Friday Agreement, signed in 1998, brought an end to decades of conflict and violence in Northern Ireland. Through negotiation and compromise, the agreement established a framework for peace, reconciliation, and power-sharing among the region's communities.

10. The Peace Corps: The Peace Corps, established by President John F. Kennedy in 1961, sends volunteers to countries around the world to promote peace and development through grassroots initiatives. Peace Corps volunteers work alongside local communities to address pressing social, economic, and environmental challenges, fostering understanding and cooperation across cultures.

These examples demonstrate the power of individuals, movements, and institutions to promote peace, reconciliation, and social change, inspiring hope and progress in communities around the world.

EIGHT
FAMILY

Family typically refers to a group of individuals who are related by blood, marriage, or adoption and share a bond of affection, mutual support, and responsibility. Family can encompass various configurations, including nuclear families (parents and children), extended families (including grandparents, aunts, uncles, and cousins), blended families (combining members from previous relationships), and chosen families (individuals who may not be related by blood but share close bonds).

Family plays a central role in shaping individuals' identities, values, and social connections. It provides a source of love, care, and emotional support, as well as a framework for socialization and interpersonal relationships. Family members often share experiences, traditions, and memories, and may collaborate on important decisions, responsibilities, and goals. Overall, family serves as a fundamental unit of society and a primary source of belonging, connection, and belonging for individuals.

Composition

Nuclear Family: Consists of two parents (mother and father) and their children.

Extended Family: Includes relatives beyond the nuclear family, such as grandparents, aunts, uncles, and cousins, who may live together or maintain close relationships.

Single-Parent Family: One parent raising one or more children.

Blended Family: Formed when two families come together due to remarriage, including step-parents and step-siblings.

Childless Family: A couple without children, often focusing on each other and their careers or other pursuits.

Adoptive Family: Includes one or more children who have been adopted.

Chosen Family: Non-biological kinship bonds, often found in communities or close friend groups that function similarly to traditional family structures.

Functions

Emotional Support: Families provide love, care, and emotional stability.

Socialization: Families teach social norms, values, and culture, shaping members' behavior and attitudes.

Economic Support: Families often share resources and provide financial support.

Reproduction and Care: Families are responsible for bearing and raising children.

Identity and Belonging: Families provide a sense of identity and belonging, creating a foundation for personal development.

Roles and Relationships

Parental Roles: Parents or guardians typically provide care, guidance, and discipline.

Sibling Relationships: Brothers and sisters often share close bonds, support each other, and sometimes engage in rivalry.

Extended Relationships: Relationships with grandparents, aunts, uncles, and cousins can provide additional support and connection.

Cultural and Legal Aspects

Cultural Definitions: Different cultures have varying definitions and structures of family, influenced by traditions, customs, and societal norms.

Legal Definitions: Legal definitions of family can affect rights, responsibilities, and entitlements, such as inheritance, custody, and social benefits.

Modern Variations

Same-Sex Families: Families with same-sex parents raising children.

Co-parenting: Parents who are not romantically involved but collaborate to raise their children.

Communal Living: Groups of individuals living together and sharing responsibilities, sometimes forming non-traditional family units.

The importance of family cannot be overstated, as it serves as the foundation of society and plays a crucial role in individuals' lives in numerous ways. Here are some key reasons why family is important:

1. Emotional Support: Family provides a source of unconditional love, acceptance, and emotional support. During challenging times, family members offer comfort, encouragement, and empathy, helping individuals

navigate difficulties and cope with stress.

2. Sense of Belonging: Family offers a sense of belonging and identity. Being part of a family provides individuals with a connection to their heritage, traditions, and cultural values, fostering a sense of continuity and rootedness.

3. Socialization and Values: Family plays a central role in socializing individuals and instilling values, beliefs, and moral principles. Through interactions with family members, individuals learn important life skills, interpersonal dynamics, and cultural norms that shape their behavior and worldview.

4. Stability and Security: Family provides a stable and secure environment for individuals to grow and thrive. A supportive family structure offers protection, stability, and a sense of safety, allowing individuals to pursue their goals and aspirations with confidence.

5. Health and Well-being: Strong family relationships are associated with better physical and mental health outcomes. Research suggests that individuals with supportive family networks experience lower levels of stress, depression, and anxiety, and have better overall health and longevity.

6. Child Development: Family plays a critical role in children's development and upbringing. A nurturing family environment promotes positive cognitive, emotional, and social development, laying the foundation for future success and well-being.

7. Intergenerational Relationships: Family facilitates meaningful intergenerational relationships, allowing individuals to connect with older and younger family members. These relationships offer opportunities for learning, mentorship, and the passing down of knowledge, traditions, and values across generations.

8. Shared Memories and Traditions: Family provides a context for creating shared memories, experiences, and traditions. Celebrating holidays, milestones, and special occasions with family members fosters a sense of unity, cohesion, and connection.

9. Mutual Support and Care: Family members often rely on each other for practical assistance, caregiving, and mutual support. Whether it's helping with childcare, providing financial assistance, or offering a listening ear, family members come together to support each other through life's challenges and transitions.

10. Long-Term Relationships: Family relationships are typically enduring and long-lasting, providing a sense of continuity and connection across

the lifespan. These enduring bonds offer comfort, companionship, and companionship, enriching individuals' lives and contributing to their overall happiness and fulfillment.

Family is a cornerstone of society and a fundamental source of love, support, and belonging for individuals. Its importance lies in providing emotional support, fostering socialization, promoting stability and well-being, and preserving cultural heritage and traditions across generations. Family relationships contribute to individuals' happiness, resilience, and overall quality of life, making them essential for personal and societal flourishing.

Family provides a multitude of benefits that contribute to individuals' overall well-being and quality of life. Here are some key benefits of family:

1. Emotional Support: Family members offer unconditional love, acceptance, and encouragement, providing a source of emotional support during times of joy, sadness, or difficulty.

2. Sense of Belonging: Being part of a family provides individuals with a sense of identity, connection, and belonging, fostering a feeling of security and rootedness.

3. Stability and Security: Family offers a stable and secure environment where individuals can feel safe and protected, allowing them to pursue their goals and aspirations with confidence.

4. Socialization and Values: Family plays a central role in socializing individuals and imparting values, beliefs, and cultural traditions that shape their worldview and behavior.

5. Health and Well-being: Strong family relationships are associated with better physical and mental health outcomes, including lower levels of stress, depression, and anxiety.

6. Child Development: A nurturing family environment promotes positive cognitive, emotional, and social development in children, laying the foundation for their future success and well-being.

7. Intergenerational Relationships: Family facilitates meaningful connections between generations, allowing individuals to learn from and bond with older and younger family members.

8. Shared Memories and Traditions: Celebrating holidays, milestones, and special occasions with family members creates lasting memories and strengthens family bonds.

9. Mutual Support and Care: Family members provide practical assistance, caregiving, and mutual support to each other, helping navigate

life's challenges and transitions.

10. Long-Term Relationships: Family relationships are enduring and long-lasting, offering companionship, companionship, and a sense of continuity across the lifespan.

Family provides a supportive and nurturing environment where individuals can grow, thrive, and find meaning and fulfillment in their lives. The benefits of family extend beyond individual well-being, contributing to the cohesion and resilience of society as a whole.

While family can provide numerous benefits, it's important to acknowledge that there can also be disadvantages or challenges associated with family dynamics. Here are some potential drawbacks of family:

1. Conflict and Tension: Family relationships can sometimes be marked by conflict, tension, and disagreements. Differences in personalities, values, and opinions may lead to arguments, misunderstandings, or strained relationships.

2. Lack of Privacy: Living in close proximity with family members can result in a lack of privacy and personal space. Individuals may feel suffocated or intruded upon, especially in households with limited physical space.

3. Dependency: Family relationships can foster dependency, particularly in situations where individuals rely heavily on family members for financial support, caregiving, or decision-making. This dependency may inhibit personal growth and autonomy.

4. Expectations and Pressure: Family expectations and pressure to conform to familial norms or traditions can create stress and tension for individuals who feel constrained or stifled by these expectations. This may lead to feelings of resentment or frustration.

5. Communication Issues: Poor communication within families can hinder understanding, connection, and problem-solving. Miscommunication, lack of listening, or unspoken tensions may exacerbate conflicts and strain relationships.

6. Interpersonal Dynamics: Complex interpersonal dynamics within families, such as sibling rivalry, favoritism, or power struggles, can create tension and discord, impacting individual well-being and family cohesion.

7. Inherited Trauma: Family histories of trauma, dysfunction, or unresolved issues may impact current family dynamics and relationships. Inherited trauma patterns or unresolved conflicts from previous generations can manifest in present-day family interactions.

8. Role Expectations: Traditional gender roles or expectations within families may limit individuals' opportunities for personal expression or fulfillment. Expectations regarding caregiving, household responsibilities, or career choices may create feelings of constraint or inequality.

9. Incompatibility: Not all family members may get along or share similar values, interests, or personalities. Incompatible family dynamics or strained relationships may lead to feelings of alienation or isolation within the family unit.

10. Boundary Issues: Unclear or porous boundaries within families can lead to enmeshment or codependency, where individual identities become intertwined or overshadowed by family dynamics. This lack of boundaries may inhibit personal autonomy and healthy individuation.

It's important to recognize that family dynamics vary widely and that not all families experience these disadvantages to the same degree. Addressing challenges within family relationships may require open communication, boundary-setting, and seeking outside support or counseling when necessary. Despite the potential drawbacks, many families are able to navigate challenges and cultivate strong, supportive relationships that contribute to individual and collective well-being.

Improving family relationships requires effort, communication, and a commitment to understanding and supporting one another. Here are some strategies to strengthen family bonds and foster positive relationships:

1. Open Communication: Encourage open and honest communication within the family. Create opportunities for family members to express their thoughts, feelings, and concerns without fear of judgment or reprisal. Active listening and empathy are key components of effective communication.

2. Quality Time Together: Make time for regular family activities and bonding experiences. Schedule family meals, outings, game nights, or other shared activities that allow family members to connect, have fun, and create lasting memories together.

3. Respect and Empathy: Foster a culture of respect, empathy, and understanding within the family. Encourage family members to listen to each other's perspectives, validate feelings, and show empathy towards one another's experiences and challenges.

4. Set Boundaries: Establish clear boundaries and expectations within the family to promote mutual respect and autonomy. Respect each other's personal space, privacy, and individual preferences, and communicate openly about boundaries and needs.

5. Resolve Conflict Constructively: Address conflicts or disagreements in a constructive and respectful manner. Practice conflict resolution techniques such as active listening, seeking compromise, and finding solutions together. Avoid blaming, criticism, or escalation of conflicts.

6. Celebrate Achievements: Acknowledge and celebrate each other's accomplishments, milestones, and successes. Show appreciation and support for family members' efforts and achievements, no matter how big or small.

7. Forgiveness and Letting Go: Practice forgiveness and let go of grudges or past resentments that may be impacting family relationships. Recognize that everyone makes mistakes and focus on moving forward with understanding and compassion.

8. Support Each Other: Be there for one another during challenging times and provide emotional support and encouragement. Offer assistance, practical help, or a listening ear when family members are facing difficulties or setbacks.

9. Family Meetings: Hold regular family meetings to discuss important topics, make decisions together, and address any issues or concerns that arise. Create a safe and inclusive environment where everyone has a voice and feels heard and valued.

10. Seek Professional Help: If family relationships are strained or facing significant challenges, consider seeking the guidance of a family therapist or counselor. Professional intervention can provide tools, strategies, and support to help improve communication, resolve conflicts, and strengthen family bonds.

By implementing these strategies and fostering a culture of respect, communication, and support, families can cultivate stronger, healthier relationships and create a nurturing and harmonious family environment.

Indian family bonds are often characterized by strong, close-knit relationships built on mutual respect, love, and shared responsibilities. Here are some great examples of how these bonds manifest in Indian families:

Intergenerational Living

Joint Families: Many Indian families live in joint family setups, where multiple generations live under one roof. This arrangement fosters deep relationships and mutual support among family members.

Elders' Wisdom: Grandparents play a significant role in imparting cultural values, traditions, and wisdom to younger generations, strengthening family ties.

Celebrations and Rituals

Festivals: Festivals like Diwali, Holi, Eid, and Christmas are celebrated with great enthusiasm, bringing family members together to share joy, perform rituals, and strengthen bonds.

Rituals and Traditions: Regular participation in rituals and traditions, such as daily prayers, family meals, and seasonal customs, reinforces a sense of belonging and unity.

Support Systems

Emotional Support: Indian families are known for their emotional support systems, where members come together to provide comfort and assistance during challenging times.

Financial Support: Family members often support each other financially, whether it's funding education, starting a business, or helping in times of need.

Parenting and Childcare

Collective Childcare: In many Indian families, childcare is a collective responsibility, with grandparents, aunts, uncles, and older siblings actively participating in raising children.

Respect for Elders: Children are taught to respect and care for their elders, fostering a sense of responsibility and gratitude.

Celebratory Milestones

Weddings: Indian weddings are grand affairs that bring together extended family members from near and far, creating lasting memories and strengthening relationships.

Birthdays and Anniversaries: Celebrating birthdays and anniversaries with family gatherings reinforces bonds and creates shared experiences.

Daily Interactions

Family Meals: Sharing meals together is a common practice that provides an opportunity for family members to connect and communicate daily.

Shared Responsibilities: Household responsibilities are often shared, teaching cooperation, respect, and understanding among family members.

Communication and Conflict Resolution

Open Communication: Many Indian families encourage open communication, where family members feel comfortable expressing their thoughts and feelings.

Conflict Resolution: Family disputes are often resolved through discussions, mediation by elders, and a focus on maintaining harmony.

Great examples of family can be found in various contexts, from real-life families to fictional portrayals in literature, film, and television. Here are some examples:

1. The Obamas: Former President Barack Obama, his wife Michelle, and their two daughters, Malia and Sasha, are often cited as a great example of a close-knit and loving family. They have consistently demonstrated strong family values, mutual respect, and support for each other, even in the spotlight of public life.

2. The Weasley Family (Harry Potter series): The Weasley family from J.K. Rowling's Harry Potter series is celebrated for their warmth, humor, and unwavering loyalty to one another. Despite facing numerous challenges and dangers, the Weasleys stand by each other's side, offering love, encouragement, and protection.

3. The Ingalls Family (Little House on the Prairie): Based on the real-life experiences of author Laura Ingalls Wilder, the Ingalls family embodies the pioneering spirit and resilience of early American settlers. Through hardships and triumphs, the Ingalls family remains united by love, faith, and a deep connection to the land.

4. The Huxtable Family (The Cosby Show): The Huxtable family, led by parents Cliff and Clair Huxtable, is renowned for their positive portrayal of an affluent African American family. With humor, warmth, and strong family values, they navigate the challenges of everyday life while nurturing close relationships and mutual respect.

5. The March Sisters (Little Women): Louisa May Alcott's classic novel Little Women follows the lives of the March sisters—Meg, Jo, Beth, and Amy—as they grow up together during the Civil War era. Despite their differences in personality, the sisters share a deep bond of sisterhood and support, demonstrating the power of family love and unity.

6. The Johnson Family (Black-ish): The Johnson family, featured in the television series Black-ish, provides a modern portrayal of a multigenerational African American family navigating contemporary issues. Through humor, honesty, and love, they tackle topics such as race, identity, and family dynamics with wit and authenticity.

7. The Pritchett-Dunphy Family (Modern Family): The blended Pritchett-Dunphy family from the sitcom Modern Family showcases the diversity of modern family structures and dynamics. Despite their quirks and differences, the family members share a strong bond and navigate life's ups and downs together with humor and resilience.

8. The Robinson Family (Lost in Space): The Robinson family, featured in the sci-fi series Lost in Space, exemplifies courage, resourcefulness, and familial love as they navigate the challenges of space exploration and survival on an alien planet.

9. The Gandhi Family: The Gandhi family, including Mahatma Gandhi, his wife Kasturba, and their children, played a pivotal role in India's freedom struggle. Despite facing numerous challenges and sacrifices, they remained united in their commitment to nonviolent resistance and social justice.

10. The Tendulkar Family: Sachin Tendulkar, often regarded as one of the greatest cricketers of all time, comes from a close-knit family that has supported him throughout his illustrious career. His parents, siblings, and wife have been pillars of strength and encouragement, contributing to his success both on and off the cricket field.

11.The Mahindra Family : The Mahindra Group, is another example of strong family bonds in the business world. The group's founder, Jagdish Chandra Mahindra, established a legacy that has been carried forward by successive generations, including Anand Mahindra. The family is known for their commitment to innovation, ethical practices, and social responsibility. Their close-knit relationships and collaborative efforts have helped them navigate challenges and achieve remarkable success.

12. The Kapoor-Khanna Family: The Kapoor-Khanna family, one of Bollywood's most prominent film dynasties, has produced several generations of talented actors, including Prithviraj Kapoor, Raj Kapoor, Rishi Kapoor, and Kareena Kapoor Khan. Known for their contributions to Indian cinema, the family has maintained strong bonds and a rich legacy in the film industry.

13. The Ambani Family: Led by patriarch Dhirubhai Ambani, the Ambani family has emerged as one of India's wealthiest and most influential business dynasties. Despite their vast wealth and success, the Ambanis are known for their close family ties and philanthropic endeavors, supporting various causes and initiatives across India.

14.. The Tata Family: The Tata family, founders of the Tata Group, one of India's largest and most respected conglomerates, has demonstrated a commitment to business ethics, philanthropy, and nation-building. Through generations, the Tata family has upheld the values of integrity, excellence, and social responsibility, leaving a lasting impact on Indian society.

These examples demonstrate the diversity of family experiences and dynamics, showcasing the importance of love, support,unity,tradition,value and resilience in forming strong family bonds.

NINE
GROWTH

Growth refers to the process of development, expansion, or advancement, often leading to an increase in size, capacity, knowledge, or success. Growth can occur in various domains, including personal, professional, economic, and societal.

Growth in life is essential for various reasons, encompassing personal, professional, and societal aspects. It involves the continuous process of developing and improving oneself, which leads to a more fulfilling and meaningful life. Here are some key points highlighting the importance of growth in life:

Personal Development

Self-Awareness: Growth fosters self-awareness, helping individuals understand their strengths, weaknesses, values, and beliefs.

Confidence and Self-Esteem: As people grow and achieve their goals, their confidence and self-esteem increase, enabling them to take on new challenges.

Resilience: Personal growth enhances resilience, helping individuals cope with setbacks and adversity more effectively.

Professional Development

Skill Enhancement: Continuous growth allows individuals to acquire new skills and improve existing ones, making them more competent and adaptable in their careers.

Career Advancement: Professional growth leads to better job opportunities, promotions, and career satisfaction.

Innovation and Creativity: A growth mindset encourages innovation and creativity, driving individuals to think outside the box and contribute new ideas.

Relationships

Improved Communication: Personal growth often includes developing better communication skills, which are crucial for building and maintaining healthy relationships.

Empathy and Understanding: Growth fosters empathy and understanding, allowing individuals to connect with others on a deeper level.

Conflict Resolution: As people grow, they become better at resolving conflicts constructively, leading to more harmonious relationships.

Mental and Emotional Well-being

Happiness and Fulfillment: Growth leads to a sense of achievement and purpose, contributing to overall happiness and life satisfaction.

Emotional Regulation: Personal development helps individuals manage their emotions better, reducing stress and improving mental health.

Mindfulness and Presence: Growth often involves mindfulness practices, which enhance one's ability to live in the present moment and appreciate life.

Societal Contribution

Positive Impact: As individuals grow and develop, they are better equipped to make positive contributions to society, whether through their work, volunteer efforts, or social interactions.

Leadership and Influence: Growth enables individuals to become effective leaders and influencers, inspiring others and driving collective progress.

Community Building: Personal growth fosters a sense of community and collaboration, as individuals work together towards common goals and societal improvement.

Continuous Learning

Lifelong Learning: Embracing growth encourages a lifelong learning mindset, keeping individuals curious, open-minded, and intellectually engaged.

Adaptability: Continuous learning and growth make individuals more adaptable to change, whether in their personal lives, careers, or the broader world.

Knowledge and Wisdom: Growth leads to the accumulation of knowledge and wisdom, enabling individuals to make informed decisions and navigate life more effectively.

Overcoming Limitations

Breaking Barriers: Growth helps individuals overcome personal limitations, fears, and self-doubt, unlocking their full potential.

Expanding Comfort Zones: Embracing growth involves stepping out of comfort zones, leading to new experiences, perspectives, and opportunities.

Setting and Achieving Goals: Growth encourages individuals to set and pursue goals, providing direction and motivation in life.

Growth in life is vital for personal fulfillment, professional success, and societal progress. It enables individuals to become the best versions of themselves, contributing positively to their own lives and the world around them. Embracing growth fosters resilience, adaptability, and a continuous quest for improvement, leading to a more enriched and meaningful life.

Here are some key aspects of growth:

1. Personal Growth: Personal growth involves the continuous development and improvement of individuals' skills, abilities, and character traits. It encompasses self-awareness, self-improvement, and self-actualization, as individuals strive to reach their full potential and lead fulfilling lives.

2. Professional Growth: Professional growth entails the advancement of one's career, skills, and expertise in the workplace. It may involve acquiring new qualifications, gaining experience, taking on greater responsibilities, and achieving career milestones.

3. Economic Growth: Economic growth refers to the increase in a country's production of goods and services over time. It is typically measured by indicators such as gross domestic product (GDP), employment rates, and per capita income, reflecting improvements in living standards and economic prosperity.

4. Organizational Growth: Organizational growth involves the expansion and development of businesses, institutions, or other entities. It may include increasing market share, expanding operations into new markets, diversifying product lines, or enhancing organizational capabilities.

5. Intellectual Growth: Intellectual growth encompasses the acquisition of knowledge, understanding, and critical thinking skills. It involves continuous learning, curiosity, and intellectual exploration, leading to broader perspectives and deeper insights.

6. Emotional and Spiritual Growth: Emotional and spiritual growth involve the cultivation of inner well-being, resilience, and connection to higher values or principles. It encompasses emotional intelligence, empathy, compassion, and spiritual fulfillment, contributing to overall happiness and

fulfillment.

7. Social Growth: Social growth involves the development of relationships, connections, and social skills. It includes building networks, fostering meaningful connections with others, and contributing positively to communities and society.

Growth is a dynamic and multifaceted process that encompasses various dimensions of human development and progress. It reflects the innate drive for improvement, evolution, and advancement that is fundamental to individual, organizational, and societal success.

Growth offers numerous benefits that contribute to personal, professional, and overall well-being. Here are some key benefits of growth:

1. Self-Improvement: Growth enables individuals to continuously improve themselves, both personally and professionally. By acquiring new skills, knowledge, and experiences, individuals enhance their capabilities and effectiveness in various aspects of life.

2. Increased Confidence: Achieving growth milestones and overcoming challenges boosts self-confidence and self-esteem. As individuals progress and develop, they gain a greater sense of self-assurance and belief in their abilities.

3. Expanded Opportunities: Growth opens up new opportunities for advancement, success, and fulfillment. Whether in career advancement, personal relationships, or other areas of life, growth expands individuals' options and possibilities for the future.

4. Adaptability: Growth fosters adaptability and resilience in the face of change and uncertainty. Individuals who embrace growth are better equipped to navigate challenges, overcome obstacles, and thrive in dynamic environments.

5. Enhanced Problem-Solving Skills: Growth involves learning from experiences and developing critical thinking and problem-solving skills. Individuals who prioritize growth are better equipped to tackle complex challenges, find creative solutions, and make informed decisions.

6. Improved Relationships: Personal growth often leads to enhanced communication, empathy, and interpersonal skills, strengthening relationships with others. Individuals who invest in their growth are better equipped to build and maintain healthy, fulfilling relationships.

7. Career Advancement: Professional growth can lead to greater job satisfaction, increased earning potential, and career advancement opportunities. Continuous learning, skill development, and networking

enhance individuals' competitiveness in the job market.

8. Increased Resilience: Growth fosters resilience and the ability to bounce back from setbacks and failures. Individuals who embrace growth see challenges as opportunities for learning and growth, rather than insurmountable obstacles.

9. Sense of Purpose: Pursuing growth gives individuals a sense of purpose and direction in life. Setting and achieving goals, pursuing passions, and striving for personal excellence provide a sense of fulfillment and satisfaction.

10. Overall Well-Being: Ultimately, growth contributes to individuals' overall well-being and quality of life. By investing in their personal and professional development, individuals experience greater happiness, fulfillment, and life satisfaction.

Growth is essential for individuals' personal and professional fulfillment, enabling them to reach their full potential and lead meaningful, purposeful lives.

While growth offers numerous benefits, there can also be potential disadvantages or challenges associated with it. Here are some drawbacks of growth:

1. Stress and Pressure: Pursuing growth can sometimes lead to increased stress and pressure, particularly when individuals set high expectations for themselves or face external pressures to succeed. The pursuit of growth may come with deadlines, competition, or performance demands that can be overwhelming.

2. Risk of Burnout: Continuous growth may lead to burnout if individuals push themselves too hard or neglect their physical, emotional, and mental well-being. Overworking, neglecting self-care, and prioritizing growth at the expense of rest and relaxation can lead to exhaustion and burnout.

3. Overemphasis on Materialism: In some cases, growth may be equated with material success or accumulation of wealth, leading to a focus on external achievements rather than internal fulfillment. This emphasis on materialism can result in a sense of emptiness or dissatisfaction, as individuals pursue growth for the wrong reasons.

4. Loss of Work-Life Balance: Pursuing growth may require significant time and energy investment, leading to a neglect of other important areas of life such as family, relationships, and personal interests. Striking a balance between personal and professional growth, as well as maintaining boundaries, is essential to prevent burnout and maintain overall well-being.

5. Fear of Failure: The pursuit of growth often involves taking risks and stepping outside of one's comfort zone, which can trigger fear of failure or rejection. This fear may hold individuals back from fully embracing growth opportunities and exploring their full potential.

6. Comparison and Self-Doubt: Engaging in a culture of constant growth and self-improvement may lead individuals to compare themselves to others and experience feelings of inadequacy or self-doubt. Constantly measuring oneself against external benchmarks or standards can erode self-confidence and hinder personal growth.

7. Loss of Authenticity: In the quest for growth, individuals may feel pressure to conform to societal expectations or mold themselves into someone they are not. This can result in a loss of authenticity and personal identity, as individuals prioritize external validation over inner fulfillment.

8. Neglect of Present Moment: Constantly striving for future growth goals may lead individuals to overlook the importance of living in the present moment and appreciating what they have accomplished thus far. Focusing too much on future aspirations can detract from enjoying the journey and finding contentment in the present.

9. Impact on Relationships: Pursuing growth may strain relationships with family, friends, or colleagues if individuals prioritize their personal or professional ambitions over nurturing meaningful connections. Balancing personal growth with maintaining healthy relationships requires effective communication and time management.

10. Sustainability Concerns: In some cases, unchecked growth may lead to environmental degradation, resource depletion, or social inequality. Sustainable growth practices that consider the long-term impact on people and the planet are essential for creating a more equitable and resilient society.

Growth is essential for personal and professional development, it's important to approach it mindfully and consider the potential drawbacks or challenges along the way. Striking a balance between ambition and well-being is key to fostering sustainable growth and fulfillment in life.

Increasing growth involves intentional efforts to develop and expand in various aspects of life. Here are some strategies to foster growth:

1. Set Clear Goals: Define specific, measurable, and achievable goals for personal, professional, and other areas of growth. Establishing clear objectives provides direction and motivation to work towards desired outcomes.

2. Continuous Learning: Cultivate a mindset of lifelong learning and curiosity. Seek out opportunities to acquire new knowledge, skills, and experiences through formal education, workshops, seminars, online courses, reading, and mentorship.

3. Step Out of Your Comfort Zone: Embrace challenges and opportunities that push you out of your comfort zone. Growth often occurs when you take risks, confront obstacles, and overcome limitations. Be open to trying new things and learning from failure.

4. Seek Feedback: Solicit feedback from peers, mentors, or supervisors to gain insights into areas for improvement and growth. Actively listen to constructive criticism and use it as a catalyst for personal and professional development.

5. Reflect and Evaluate: Regularly reflect on your progress and experiences to assess what is working well and where adjustments are needed. Set aside time for self-reflection, journaling, or meditation to gain clarity and insight into your goals and aspirations.

6. Embrace Change: Be adaptable and resilient in the face of change and uncertainty. View challenges as opportunities for growth and transformation, rather than obstacles to be avoided. Cultivate a growth mindset that sees setbacks as learning opportunities.

7. Expand Your Network: Surround yourself with diverse and supportive individuals who inspire and challenge you to grow. Build relationships with people who have different perspectives, backgrounds, and expertise, and leverage their knowledge and experiences to broaden your own.

8. Invest in Personal Development: Allocate time, resources, and energy towards your personal growth and well-being. Practice self-care, prioritize your health and wellness, and engage in activities that nourish your mind, body, and spirit.

9. Set Priorities: Identify your priorities and focus on activities that align with your values, goals, and long-term aspirations. Learn to say no to distractions or commitments that detract from your growth and well-being.

10. Celebrate Achievements: Acknowledge and celebrate your successes, milestones, and progress along the way. Recognize the effort and dedication you put into your growth journey, and use positive reinforcement to maintain momentum and motivation.

By incorporating these strategies into your daily life and mindset, you can create an environment that fosters growth, development, and fulfillment in all areas of your life.

Great examples of growth can be found in various contexts, from individuals overcoming personal challenges to organizations achieving significant milestones. Here are some inspiring examples:

1. Elon Musk: The founder and CEO of SpaceX, Tesla, Neuralink, and The Boring Company, Elon Musk is renowned for his visionary approach to innovation and entrepreneurship. His relentless pursuit of ambitious goals, such as colonizing Mars and revolutionizing transportation, demonstrates a commitment to continuous growth and advancement in technology and space exploration.

2. Malala Yousafzai: Malala Yousafzai is a Pakistani activist for female education and the youngest Nobel Prize laureate. Despite facing adversity and violence for her advocacy, Malala continued to fight for girls' right to education, becoming a global symbol of courage, resilience, and empowerment. Her unwavering commitment to education and social change embodies the power of personal growth and activism.

3. Apple Inc.: Apple Inc. is a prime example of organizational growth and innovation in the technology industry. From its humble beginnings in a garage to becoming one of the world's most valuable companies, Apple has consistently pushed the boundaries of design, technology, and user experience. Through products like the iPhone, iPad, and Mac, Apple has transformed industries and revolutionized the way we communicate, work, and live.

4. Nelson Mandela: Nelson Mandela, South Africa's first black president and a global icon of reconciliation and justice, exemplifies the power of personal and societal growth. After spending 27 years in prison for his anti-apartheid activism, Mandela emerged as a statesman committed to forgiveness, reconciliation, and building a democratic South Africa. His journey from prisoner to president reflects the transformative potential of resilience, forgiveness, and moral growth.

5. Greta Thunberg: Greta Thunberg is a Swedish environmental activist who gained international prominence for her efforts to address climate change. Through her school strikes and impassioned speeches, she has galvanized a global movement of young people demanding action on climate justice. Greta's courage, determination, and unwavering commitment to environmental activism inspire others to advocate for positive change and environmental sustainability.

6. Warby Parker: Warby Parker is a direct-to-consumer eyewear company that disrupted the traditional eyewear industry with its innovative business

model and social mission. Founded by four friends as a response to the high cost of eyewear, Warby Parker has grown into a successful business that combines affordable, stylish eyewear with a commitment to social impact through its "Buy a Pair, Give a Pair" program. The company's growth exemplifies the power of entrepreneurship, innovation, and social responsibility.

7. Serena Williams: Serena Williams is widely regarded as one of the greatest tennis players of all time. Throughout her career, she has continually pushed herself to achieve new heights in the sport, breaking records and overcoming setbacks along the way. Serena's dedication, resilience, and relentless pursuit of excellence serve as a testament to the power of growth mindset and perseverance in sports and life.

8. Ratan Tata: Ratan Tata, the former chairman of Tata Sons, is known for his transformative leadership and vision for the Tata Group. Under his stewardship, the Tata Group expanded globally, diversified its portfolio, and became one of India's most respected conglomerates. Ratan Tata's commitment to innovation, social responsibility, and ethical business practices has been instrumental in driving the growth and success of the Tata Group.

9. Reliance Industries Limited (RIL): Founded by Dhirubhai Ambani, Reliance Industries Limited (RIL) has grown into one of India's largest and most valuable companies. Under the leadership of Mukesh Ambani, RIL has diversified its business interests across sectors such as petrochemicals, refining, telecommunications, and retail. RIL's rapid growth and expansion have played a significant role in India's economic development and industrial progress.

10. ISRO (Indian Space Research Organisation): ISRO has achieved remarkable growth and success in space exploration and satellite technology. From launching its first satellite, Aryabhata, in 1975 to conducting successful Mars and Moon missions, ISRO has demonstrated India's prowess in space research and technology. ISRO's achievements have placed India among the leading space-faring nations in the world and have contributed to advancements in communication, navigation, and remote sensing technologies.

11. Infosys: Founded by Narayana Murthy and his colleagues, Infosys is one of India's leading multinational corporations in the IT sector. Infosys' journey from a small start-up to a global powerhouse is a testament to its focus on innovation, quality, and customer-centricity. Infosys has played a

pivotal role in India's IT revolution and has contributed significantly to job creation, skill development, and economic growth.

12. Kiran Mazumdar-Shaw: Kiran Mazumdar-Shaw is the founder and chairperson of Biocon Limited, India's largest pharmaceutical company. As a pioneering entrepreneur in the biotechnology industry, Kiran Mazumdar-Shaw has led Biocon's growth into a global leader in biosimilars and research-driven pharmaceuticals. Her leadership and vision have contributed to India's emergence as a hub for biotechnology innovation and entrepreneurship.

13. Uday Kotak: Uday Kotak is the founder and CEO of Kotak Mahindra Bank, one of India's leading private sector banks. Under his leadership, Kotak Mahindra Bank has experienced rapid growth and expansion, becoming one of the country's most trusted financial institutions. Uday Kotak's entrepreneurial spirit, strategic acumen, and focus on customer service have propelled the bank's success and prominence in the Indian banking industry.

These examples demonstrate the diverse ways in which individuals and organizations can pursue growth, achieve success, and make a positive impact on the world. Whether through personal resilience, innovation, social activism, or business entrepreneurship, growth is a powerful force for positive change and advancement.They serve as inspiration for future generations of Global leaders and entrepreneurs striving to make a positive impact on society and the economy.

TEN
VARIETY

"Varieties" refers to different types, forms, or kinds of something. It indicates the existence of diversity or multiplicity within a particular category or group. For example, the term can be used to describe the different varieties of a plant species, the various flavors of a food product, or the diverse approaches to solving a problem. "Varieties" can also refer to distinctions or differences within a broader context, highlighting the range of options or alternatives available.

Variety in personal life refers to incorporating diverse experiences, activities, and perspectives into one's daily routine and lifestyle. Embracing variety can enrich your life, stimulate growth, and increase overall happiness and satisfaction. Here are some key aspects of incorporating variety in personal life:

Experiences

Travel: Visiting new places, whether local or international, exposes you to different cultures, environments, and lifestyles.

Hobbies and Interests: Engaging in various hobbies and interests, such as sports, arts, music, cooking, or gardening, can provide enjoyment and broaden your skills.

Social Activities: Participating in different social activities, like joining clubs, attending events, or meeting new people, can enhance your social network and introduce you to new perspectives.

Learning and Development

Education: Pursuing different educational opportunities, such as online courses, workshops, or formal education, can expand your knowledge and skillset.

Reading: Reading a wide range of books, articles, and other materials can expose you to new ideas and viewpoints.

Challenges: Taking on various challenges and stepping out of your comfort zone can promote personal growth and resilience.

Perspectives

Cultural Exposure: Learning about and appreciating different cultures, traditions, and languages can broaden your worldview and promote tolerance and understanding.

Diverse Relationships: Building relationships with people from different backgrounds, professions, and life experiences can provide new insights and enrich your personal life.

Open-mindedness: Being open to new ideas, experiences, and perspectives can lead to a more adaptable and flexible mindset.

Routine and Lifestyle

Daily Routine: Introducing variety into your daily routine, such as changing your exercise regimen, trying new foods, or altering your commute, can prevent monotony and keep life interesting.

Creative Activities: Engaging in creative activities, like painting, writing, or crafting, can stimulate your imagination and provide a sense of accomplishment.

Exploring Nature: Spending time in different natural settings, such as parks, beaches, mountains, or forests, can refresh your mind and body.

Relationships and Social Interactions

Meeting New People: Actively seeking opportunities to meet new people can introduce you to different viewpoints and experiences.

Networking: Expanding your professional and personal network can open up new opportunities and enrich your social life.

Family and Friends: Spending quality time with family and friends and participating in diverse activities can strengthen relationships and create lasting memories.

Variety in personal life is important for several reasons:

1. Stimulation and Engagement: Variety keeps life interesting and prevents boredom. Engaging in a variety of activities, hobbies, and experiences stimulates the mind and provides opportunities for learning, growth, and creativity.

2. Prevention of Burnout: Doing the same thing repetitively can lead to burnout and fatigue. Variety allows individuals to switch between different tasks or activities, preventing monotony and helping maintain motivation

and energy levels.

3. Exploration and Discovery: Variety encourages exploration and discovery. Trying new things, visiting new places, and meeting new people can broaden horizons, expand perspectives, and foster personal development.

4. Flexibility and Adaptability: Embracing variety enhances flexibility and adaptability. Individuals who are accustomed to diverse experiences and situations are better equipped to handle change, uncertainty, and unexpected challenges in life.

5. Enhanced Well-Being: Variety contributes to overall well-being by promoting balance and fulfillment. Balancing work, leisure, relationships, and personal interests allows individuals to lead more satisfying and meaningful lives.

6. Personal Growth: Variety fosters personal growth by exposing individuals to different perspectives, ideas, and opportunities. Embracing diversity in experiences and interactions can lead to greater self-awareness, resilience, and personal transformation.

7. Improved Relationships: Variety in personal life can enrich relationships with others. Sharing diverse experiences, interests, and conversations with friends, family, and partners strengthens bonds and fosters deeper connections.

8. Cognitive Benefits: Engaging in a variety of mental activities, such as learning new skills, solving puzzles, or exploring different topics, provides cognitive benefits. It helps maintain cognitive function, memory, and mental agility as individuals age.

9. Emotional Well-Being: Variety can positively impact emotional well-being by providing opportunities for enjoyment, relaxation, and fulfillment. Having a diverse range of activities and experiences to draw upon can help individuals cope with stress, anxiety, and negative emotions.

10. Sense of Fulfillment: Embracing variety in personal life contributes to a sense of fulfillment and satisfaction. Achieving a balance between different aspects of life, pursuing passions and interests, and experiencing new things can lead to a richer and more meaningful existence.

In summary, variety in personal life is essential for maintaining balance, preventing stagnation, and promoting growth and well-being. Embracing diversity in experiences, activities, and relationships enriches life and enhances its quality and meaning.

Variety in personal life offers numerous benefits that contribute to overall well-being and fulfillment. Here are some key advantages:

1. Increased Resilience: Variety builds resilience by exposing individuals to different challenges and experiences. It helps develop coping skills and adaptability, enabling individuals to bounce back from setbacks and thrive in the face of adversity.

2. Joy and Enjoyment: Variety adds joy and enjoyment to life by offering a range of experiences and opportunities for fun and recreation. Whether it's trying new foods, exploring new hobbies, or traveling to new destinations, variety enriches life with moments of pleasure and happiness.

3. Stimulation and Interest: Variety adds excitement and interest to life by introducing new experiences, activities, and challenges. It prevents monotony and boredom, keeping individuals engaged and motivated to explore and learn.

4. Personal Growth: Experiencing a variety of situations and activities promotes personal growth and development. It encourages individuals to step out of their comfort zones, learn new skills, and broaden their perspectives, leading to greater self-awareness and resilience.

5. Enhanced Creativity: Exposure to diverse experiences stimulates creativity and innovation. Engaging in different activities and exploring new ideas encourages individuals to think outside the box, fostering creativity and problem-solving skills.

6. Adaptability: Embracing variety enhances adaptability and flexibility in navigating life's challenges and changes. Individuals who are accustomed to diverse experiences are better equipped to cope with uncertainty and thrive in dynamic environments.

7. Improved Relationships: Variety in personal life enriches relationships with others. Sharing diverse experiences and interests strengthens bonds and fosters deeper connections with friends, family, and partners.

8. Emotional Well-Being: Variety contributes to emotional well-being by providing opportunities for enjoyment, relaxation, and fulfillment. Engaging in a variety of activities promotes a balanced lifestyle and helps individuals cope with stress and negative emotions.

9. Sense of Fulfillment: Variety enhances the sense of fulfillment and satisfaction in life. Achieving a balance between different aspects of life, pursuing passions and interests, and experiencing new things lead to a richer and more meaningful existence.

10. Brain Health: Exposure to a variety of mental stimuli promotes brain health and cognitive function. Engaging in diverse activities, such as learning new skills or exploring different topics, helps maintain mental agility and memory as individuals age.

11. Increased Resilience: Variety builds resilience by exposing individuals to different challenges and experiences. It helps develop coping skills and adaptability, enabling individuals to bounce back from setbacks and thrive in the face of adversity.

12. Joy and Enjoyment: Variety adds joy and enjoyment to life by offering a range of experiences and opportunities for fun and recreation. Whether it's trying new foods, exploring new hobbies, or traveling to new destinations, variety enriches life with moments of pleasure and happiness.

Variety in personal life contributes to overall well-being by stimulating growth, fostering creativity, enhancing relationships, and promoting happiness and fulfillment.

While variety in personal life offers numerous benefits, it can also present some disadvantages or challenges. Here are some potential drawbacks:

1. Overwhelm and Decision Fatigue: Having too many options or commitments can lead to overwhelm and decision fatigue. Constantly juggling between different activities and responsibilities may leave individuals feeling stressed, exhausted, and unable to focus.

2. Lack of Depth or Mastery: Engaging in a wide range of activities may prevent individuals from developing depth or mastery in any one area. Constantly switching between interests or pursuits may result in shallow knowledge or skills, hindering personal growth and fulfillment.

3. Difficulty in Time Management: Managing a diverse array of commitments and activities can be challenging. Without effective time management skills, individuals may struggle to prioritize tasks, meet deadlines, or maintain a healthy work-life balance.

4. Fragmentation of Attention: Constantly shifting focus between different activities may lead to fragmented attention and reduced productivity. Individuals may find it difficult to concentrate or fully engage in any one task, leading to subpar results or unfinished projects.

5. Social Disconnection: Embracing variety in personal life may lead to social fragmentation or disconnection. Spending too much time pursuing individual interests or hobbies may detract from opportunities for social interaction and meaningful relationships with others.

6. Risk of Burnout: Overcommitting to a wide range of activities or obligations can increase the risk of burnout. Pushing oneself too hard to maintain a diverse lifestyle may lead to physical and emotional exhaustion, diminishing overall well-being and satisfaction.

7. Financial Strain: Engaging in a variety of activities or interests may incur financial costs. Constantly trying new hobbies, traveling to different destinations, or participating in various events can strain financial resources, leading to stress or debt.

8. Loss of Focus or Direction: Lack of focus or direction may result from constantly pursuing novelty or variety in personal life. Without clear goals or priorities, individuals may feel adrift or uncertain about their purpose or direction, hindering personal fulfillment and satisfaction.

9. Risk of Overcommitment: The desire to experience a wide range of activities may lead to overcommitment. Saying yes to too many obligations or opportunities may spread oneself too thin, leading to feelings of overwhelm or dissatisfaction.

10. Comparison and FOMO: Constant exposure to diverse experiences through social media or other channels may fuel comparison and fear of missing out (FOMO). Individuals may feel pressure to keep up with others' seemingly exciting or glamorous lives, leading to feelings of inadequacy or dissatisfaction with their own experiences.

While variety in personal life can enrich experiences and promote growth, it's important to balance diversity with focus, prioritization, and self-care to avoid potential disadvantages such as overwhelm, lack of depth, or social disconnection.

Improving variety in life involves intentionally seeking out and embracing diverse experiences, interests, and opportunities. Here are some strategies to enhance variety:

1. Explore New Interests: Be open to trying new activities, hobbies, and experiences that you haven't explored before. Take classes, attend workshops, or join clubs related to areas you're curious about to expand your horizons and discover new passions.

2. Step Out of Your Comfort Zone: Challenge yourself to step out of your comfort zone and try things that feel unfamiliar or intimidating. Pushing past your fears and limitations can lead to personal growth and a broader range of experiences.

3. Diversify Your Routine: Break out of monotonous routines by incorporating variety into your daily life. Mix up your schedule, try new

routes to work, or experiment with different ways of spending your free time to keep things fresh and interesting.

4. Travel to New Destinations: Traveling to new places allows you to experience different cultures, cuisines, and landscapes. Whether it's exploring a foreign country or visiting a nearby town you've never been to, travel opens up opportunities for diverse experiences and perspectives.

5. Embrace Cultural Diversity: Seek out opportunities to engage with people from diverse backgrounds and cultures. Attend cultural festivals, dine at ethnic restaurants, or participate in community events to learn about and celebrate different traditions and customs.

6. Learn Continuously: Cultivate a lifelong learning mindset by seeking out knowledge and skills in a variety of areas. Read books, watch documentaries, or take online courses on topics that interest you to broaden your understanding and expertise.

7. Mix Up Your Social Circle: Expand your social circle by connecting with people from different walks of life. Attend networking events, join social groups, or volunteer for causes you care about to meet new people and exchange ideas with individuals from diverse backgrounds.

8. Experiment with Different Foods: Explore the culinary world by trying new foods and cuisines from different cultures. Visit ethnic restaurants, experiment with cooking recipes from around the world, or attend food festivals to expand your palate and discover new flavors.

9. Attend Varied Events: Attend a variety of events and activities in your community, ranging from art exhibitions and concerts to sports games and outdoor adventures. Exploring different types of events exposes you to diverse experiences and helps you find activities you enjoy.

10. Reflect and Adapt: Regularly reflect on your experiences and preferences to identify areas where you'd like to introduce more variety. Be adaptable and open to adjusting your routines, interests, and goals based on your evolving interests and priorities.

By incorporating these strategies into your life, you can cultivate a richer and more diverse range of experiences, interests, and opportunities, leading to greater fulfillment and personal growth.

Here are some examples of variety in different areas of life:

1. Food: Cuisine from around the world provides a vast array of flavors, ingredients, and cooking styles. Whether it's spicy Indian curries, savory Italian pasta dishes, or fresh Japanese sushi, the variety of food choices allows individuals to explore different cultures and culinary traditions.

2. Travel: Traveling to different destinations offers a variety of experiences, landscapes, and cultures. From bustling cities like New York and Tokyo to serene natural wonders like the Grand Canyon and the Swiss Alps, each destination provides unique sights, sounds, and experiences for travelers to enjoy.

3. Music: The music industry offers a wide variety of genres, styles, and artists to suit diverse tastes. Whether it's classical symphonies, rock anthems, hip-hop beats, or jazz improvisations, music provides endless opportunities for individuals to discover new sounds and express themselves creatively.

4. Hobbies: Engaging in hobbies and leisure activities allows individuals to explore a variety of interests and passions. From gardening and painting to photography and sports, there are countless hobbies to choose from, providing opportunities for relaxation, creativity, and personal fulfillment.

5. Career Paths: The professional world offers a variety of career paths and opportunities for individuals with diverse skills, interests, and backgrounds. Whether it's pursuing a career in healthcare, technology, education, or the arts, individuals can choose paths that align with their passions and aspirations.

6. Books and Literature: Literature encompasses a wide variety of genres, themes, and perspectives, catering to different interests and tastes. From classic literature and contemporary fiction to non-fiction essays and poetry, books offer a rich tapestry of stories and ideas for readers to explore.

7. Fashion: Fashion reflects a diverse range of styles, trends, and expressions of personal identity. From casual streetwear and formal attire to avant-garde couture and ethnic fashion, individuals can express themselves through clothing in myriad ways, embracing their unique sense of style.

8. Social Interactions: Social interactions provide opportunities to connect with a variety of people from different backgrounds, cultures, and perspectives. Whether it's spending time with family and friends, participating in community events, or networking with colleagues, each interaction offers a chance to learn, grow, and form meaningful relationships.

9. Art and Creativity: Artistic expression encompasses a wide variety of mediums, techniques, and styles. From painting and sculpture to photography and digital media, artists can explore their creativity and share their unique perspectives with the world, enriching society with diverse forms of artistic expression.

10. Nature and Wildlife: The natural world offers a rich variety of landscapes, ecosystems, and species. From lush rainforests and vast deserts to vibrant coral reefs and snowy mountaintops, nature provides endless opportunities for exploration, discovery, and appreciation of its beauty and diversity.

These examples illustrate the abundance of variety in life, highlighting the richness and diversity of experiences, opportunities, and perspectives available to individuals.

Will Smith:

1. Acting Career: Will Smith has demonstrated remarkable versatility in his acting career, spanning a wide variety of genres and roles. He's known for his comedic performances in TV shows like "The Fresh Prince of Bel-Air," where he played a charming and witty teenager navigating life with his affluent relatives. He seamlessly transitioned into dramatic roles, such as his portrayal of real-life boxer Muhammad Ali in "Ali," showcasing his depth and range as an actor.

2. Blockbuster Films: Will Smith has starred in a diverse range of blockbuster films, showcasing his ability to excel in different genres. From action-packed thrillers like "Independence Day" and "Men in Black" to heartfelt dramas like "The Pursuit of Happyness" and "Seven Pounds," Smith has captivated audiences with his charisma and talent across various film genres.

3. Music Career: In addition to his success in acting, Will Smith has had a successful music career, demonstrating his versatility as a performer. As part of the hip-hop duo DJ Jazzy Jeff & The Fresh Prince, Smith released hit songs like "Summertime" and "Parents Just Don't Understand," showcasing his skill as a rapper and entertainer.

4. Producer and Philanthropist: Beyond his work in entertainment, Will Smith has also diversified his portfolio as a producer and philanthropist. He has produced several successful films and TV shows through his production company, Overbrook Entertainment, including "The Karate Kid" and "The Pursuit of Happyness." Additionally, Smith and his wife, Jada Pinkett Smith, are actively involved in various philanthropic endeavors, supporting causes such as education, environmental conservation, and youth empowerment.

Will Smith's career exemplifies the concept of variety, as he has successfully navigated multiple industries and roles with skill, versatility, and charisma. His ability to excel in acting, music, producing, and philanthropy highlights the power of embracing diverse opportunities and pursuing passions across different domains.

ELEVEN
EMPATHY

Empathy is the ability to understand and share the feelings, thoughts, and experiences of another person. It involves the capacity to step into someone else's shoes, to see the world from their perspective, and to genuinely connect with their emotions and struggles. Empathy goes beyond sympathy, which is merely acknowledging another person's feelings, to actively experiencing and resonating with their emotions. It's a fundamental aspect of human connection, fostering understanding, compassion, and support in relationships and interactions.

Empathy is crucial in personal life for several reasons:

1. Strengthening Relationships: Empathy allows individuals to understand and connect with others on a deeper level, fostering trust, intimacy, and emotional bonds in relationships.

2. Resolving Conflicts: By empathizing with others' perspectives and emotions, individuals can navigate disagreements and conflicts more effectively, leading to better communication and resolution.

3. Providing Support: Empathy enables individuals to offer genuine support and comfort to friends, family members, and loved ones during challenging times, enhancing their well-being and resilience.

4. Fostering Understanding: Empathy promotes tolerance, acceptance, and appreciation for diverse perspectives, experiences, and backgrounds, fostering a more inclusive and compassionate society.

5. Promoting Emotional Health: Engaging in empathetic interactions can improve mental and emotional well-being by reducing feelings of loneliness, isolation, and disconnection, and increasing feelings of belonging and validation.

6. Enhancing Parenting Skills: Empathetic parents are better able to understand and respond to their children's needs, feelings, and behaviors, creating a nurturing and supportive family environment.

7. Cultivating Self-Awareness: Practicing empathy encourages individuals to reflect on their own emotions, biases, and experiences, fostering self-awareness and personal growth.

8. Building Trust and Respect: Empathy builds trust and respect in personal relationships by demonstrating care, consideration, and understanding for others' feelings and experiences.

9. Strengthening Social Connections: Empathetic individuals are more likely to form meaningful and fulfilling social connections, leading to greater happiness, satisfaction, and overall well-being.

10. Making a Positive Impact: Empathy empowers individuals to make a positive difference in the lives of others by offering support, kindness, and compassion, contributing to a more caring and compassionate world.

Empathy is essential for nurturing healthy, fulfilling, and meaningful relationships, fostering emotional well-being, and promoting understanding and connection in personal life.

Empathy offers numerous benefits, both for individuals and for society as a whole. Here are some of the key advantages of cultivating empathy:

1. Improved Relationships: Empathy strengthens interpersonal connections by fostering understanding, trust, and mutual respect. When people feel heard and understood, it enhances the quality of their relationships with others.

2. Enhanced Communication: Empathetic individuals are better communicators because they are attuned to the emotions and needs of others. They can convey their thoughts and feelings more effectively and respond sensitively to the communication of others.

3. Conflict Resolution: Empathy plays a crucial role in resolving conflicts peacefully and constructively. By understanding the perspectives and emotions of all parties involved, empathetic individuals can find common ground and work toward mutually beneficial solutions.

4. Increased Emotional Intelligence: Empathy is a key component of emotional intelligence, which is essential for personal and professional success. Individuals with high emotional intelligence are better equipped to navigate social situations, manage relationships, and regulate their own emotions.

5. Greater Personal Well-Being: Cultivating empathy can lead to greater personal fulfillment and well-being. By connecting with others on a deeper level and contributing to their happiness and success, empathetic individuals experience a sense of purpose and satisfaction in their lives.

6. Reduced Prejudice and Stereotyping: Empathy helps break down barriers and promote understanding across cultural, racial, and socioeconomic divides. By recognizing and appreciating the experiences and perspectives of others, people can overcome prejudice and stereotypes.

7. Enhanced Leadership Skills: Empathetic leaders are more effective at inspiring and motivating others, building cohesive teams, and fostering a positive organizational culture. They are better able to understand and address the needs and concerns of their team members.

8. Increased Compassion and Altruism: Empathy motivates people to act compassionately and altruistically toward others in need. It prompts individuals to offer support, assistance, and kindness, contributing to the well-being of individuals and communities.

9. Improved Mental Health: Empathy is associated with lower levels of stress, anxiety, and depression. By connecting with others and offering support, empathetic individuals can experience greater resilience and psychological well-being.

10. Positive Societal Impact: Empathy fosters a culture of kindness, compassion, and social responsibility. It promotes cooperation, empathy, and understanding, leading to a more harmonious and inclusive society.

Empathy is a powerful force for positive change, enriching relationships, promoting understanding, and fostering a more compassionate and equitable world.

While empathy offers numerous benefits, there are also potential disadvantages or challenges associated with it:

1. Emotional Burnout: Constantly experiencing and absorbing the emotions of others can lead to emotional exhaustion and burnout, especially for individuals in caregiving professions or roles that require frequent empathetic engagement.

2. Overidentification: Overly empathetic individuals may struggle to maintain boundaries and separate their own emotions from those of others. This can lead to becoming overly involved in others' problems or experiencing emotional distress as a result of empathizing too deeply.

3. Compassion Fatigue: Experiencing empathy for others' suffering can take a toll on mental and emotional well-being, leading to compassion fatigue. This can manifest as feelings of numbness, detachment, or apathy toward others' pain and suffering.

4. Bias and Favoritism: Empathizing more strongly with certain individuals or groups can lead to bias and favoritism in decision-making and interactions. This can undermine fairness and equality, particularly in professional or organizational settings.

5. Emotional Manipulation: Individuals with high levels of empathy may be susceptible to emotional manipulation by others who seek to exploit their compassion and kindness for their own gain. This can lead to feelings of resentment or betrayal.

6. Reduced Objectivity: Excessive empathy may cloud judgment and impair rational decision-making, as individuals prioritize emotional connections and considerations over objective facts and analysis.

7. Emotional Overload: Constant exposure to the suffering and distress of others can overwhelm empathetic individuals, leading to feelings of helplessness, anxiety, or depression.

8. Strained Relationships: Empathetic individuals may struggle to maintain healthy boundaries in relationships, leading to codependency or emotional enmeshment with others.

9. Vulnerability to Secondary Trauma: Those who frequently empathize with individuals who have experienced trauma may be at risk of experiencing secondary trauma themselves. This can have a significant impact on mental and emotional well-being.

10. Inaction or Avoidance: Overwhelmed by the pain and suffering of others, some empathetic individuals may become paralyzed or avoidant, choosing to disengage from situations or relationships that evoke strong emotional responses.

It's important to recognize these potential challenges associated with empathy and to practice self-care and boundary-setting to maintain emotional balance and well-being while still fostering compassion and understanding for others.

Developing empathy involves both self-awareness and intentional efforts to understand and connect with others. Here are some strategies to cultivate empathy:

1. Active Listening: Practice attentive listening when interacting with others. Focus on what they are saying without interrupting, and make an

effort to understand their perspective before responding.

2. Put Yourself in Their Shoes: Imagine how you would feel and react if you were in the other person's situation. This helps you develop a deeper understanding of their emotions and experiences.

3. Ask Open-Ended Questions: Encourage others to share their thoughts and feelings by asking open-ended questions that invite them to elaborate on their experiences.

4. Practice Perspective-Taking: Challenge yourself to see things from different viewpoints, especially those that differ from your own. This helps broaden your understanding of diverse perspectives and experiences.

5. Practice Empathetic Body Language: Pay attention to your body language, such as maintaining eye contact, nodding in agreement, and offering supportive gestures, to convey empathy and understanding.

6. Validate Feelings: Acknowledge and validate the emotions of others, even if you don't agree with their perspective. Let them know that their feelings are heard and respected.

7. Cultivate Curiosity: Show genuine interest in learning about others' experiences, backgrounds, and perspectives. Curiosity can lead to deeper connections and empathy.

8. Practice Self-Reflection: Reflect on your own emotions, biases, and experiences to better understand how they influence your perceptions of others. This self-awareness can enhance your ability to empathize with others.

9. Read Fiction and Watch Films: Engage with literature, films, and other media that explore diverse characters and experiences. This can broaden your perspective and increase your empathy for people from different backgrounds.

10. Volunteer and Engage in Community Service: Get involved in activities that allow you to interact with people from diverse backgrounds and experiences. Volunteering can help you develop empathy by providing opportunities to connect with and support others in need.

By incorporating these practices into your daily life, you can enhance your ability to empathize with others and cultivate deeper, more meaningful connections.

A great example of empathy is the story of Rosa Parks, often referred to as the "mother of the civil rights movement" in the United States.

In December 1955, Rosa Parks, an African American woman, was on her way home from work in Montgomery, Alabama, when she boarded a segregated bus. According to the laws of the time, African Americans were required to sit in the back of the bus while white passengers occupied the front seats. When the bus became crowded, the driver ordered Rosa Parks and three other African American passengers to give up their seats for white passengers.

Rosa Parks, however, refused to give up her seat. Her act of defiance was not simply a matter of tiredness or inconvenience; it was a deliberate act of empathy and resistance against the systemic injustice and discrimination faced by African Americans on a daily basis. Rosa Parks empathized with the struggles of her community, recognizing that giving up her seat would perpetuate the dehumanizing segregation laws that oppressed them.

Her courageous act sparked the Montgomery Bus Boycott, a pivotal moment in the civil rights movement, during which African Americans boycotted the city's buses for over a year in protest against segregation. Rosa Parks' empathy and courage inspired countless others to stand up against injustice and fight for equality and civil rights.

Rosa Parks' story serves as a powerful example of empathy in action, demonstrating how one person's willingness to empathize with the experiences of others can lead to profound social change and inspire movements for justice and equality.

One notable example of empathy demonstrated by a celebrity is the philanthropic work of Oprah Winfrey. Throughout her career, Oprah has consistently used her platform to advocate for social justice, education, and humanitarian causes, demonstrating a deep sense of empathy for those in need.

In addition to her influential talk show, where she often featured stories of individuals facing hardship and adversity, Oprah has established several charitable foundations aimed at empowering disadvantaged communities and supporting vulnerable populations.

One of her most well-known initiatives is the Oprah Winfrey Leadership Academy for Girls in South Africa. Founded in 2007, the academy provides education and leadership development opportunities to academically talented girls from disadvantaged backgrounds. Oprah's commitment to providing quality education and empowering young women reflects her empathy for those facing systemic barriers to success.

Furthermore, Oprah has been a vocal advocate for various social issues, including women's rights, racial equality, and LGBTQ+ rights. She has used her influence to raise awareness, promote dialogue, and support initiatives that address systemic injustice and inequality.

Through her philanthropy, advocacy, and personal interactions, Oprah Winfrey exemplifies empathy by demonstrating care, compassion, and a genuine concern for the well-being of others. Her actions inspire others to empathize with those facing challenges and to use their resources and influence to create positive change in the world.

TWELVE
CERTAINTY

Certainty refers to the state or quality of being definite, sure, or confident about something. It implies a lack of doubt or ambiguity, indicating a high level of confidence or conviction in the truth, accuracy, or outcome of a particular situation, belief, or proposition.

When someone is certain about something, they have a strong belief or assurance in its validity or correctness, often based on evidence, knowledge, experience, or intuition. Certainty can range from absolute conviction to a more moderate level of confidence, depending on the clarity and strength of the supporting factors.

In essence, certainty reflects a sense of assurance or conviction that something is true, accurate, or reliable, without significant room for doubt or uncertainty. It plays a crucial role in decision-making, problem-solving, and understanding the world around us, providing a foundation for confidence, action, and belief.

Life without certainty can be challenging and unpredictable. Without a sense of assurance or predictability, individuals may experience heightened anxiety, insecurity, and difficulty making decisions. Here are some aspects of life that can be affected by the absence of certainty:

1. Decision-Making: Without certainty, individuals may struggle to make decisions confidently, leading to indecision or second-guessing. The lack of clarity about potential outcomes can make it challenging to weigh options and commit to a course of action.

2. Relationships: Uncertainty in relationships can lead to insecurity and distrust, as individuals may question the reliability or intentions of others. Without clear communication and mutual understanding, conflicts and misunderstandings may arise, straining interpersonal connections.

3. Career and Financial Planning: Uncertainty in the job market or economy can make career and financial planning more difficult. Individuals may hesitate to make long-term commitments or investments without confidence in future stability or opportunities.

4. Health and Well-being: Uncertainty about health outcomes or access to healthcare can create stress and anxiety. Without certainty about the availability of resources or support, individuals may struggle to manage their physical and mental well-being effectively.

5. Goals and Aspirations: Lack of certainty can undermine individuals' confidence in pursuing their goals and aspirations. The fear of failure or unpredictability may deter them from taking risks or stepping outside their comfort zone to pursue their dreams.

6. Sense of Security: Certainty provides a sense of security and stability in life. Without it, individuals may feel vulnerable to unexpected events or challenges, leading to heightened stress and anxiety about the future.

7. Trust and Confidence: Uncertainty erodes trust and confidence in institutions, leaders, and societal structures. Without confidence in the reliability or fairness of systems, individuals may become disillusioned or cynical about their ability to effect change or achieve justice.

8. Sense of Identity: Certainty plays a role in shaping individuals' sense of identity and purpose. Without clarity about their values, beliefs, or direction in life, individuals may struggle to find meaning and fulfillment in their experiences.

9. Adaptability: While uncertainty can foster adaptability and resilience in some situations, excessive unpredictability can overwhelm individuals' ability to cope and adjust. Without a sense of certainty about their circumstances, individuals may feel powerless or overwhelmed by the challenges they face.

10. Hope and Optimism: Certainty provides a foundation for hope and optimism about the future. Without it, individuals may struggle to maintain a positive outlook or belief in the possibility of better days ahead.

Life without certainty can be unsettling and challenging, impacting various aspects of well-being, relationships, and decision-making. However, uncertainty can also present opportunities for growth, resilience, and adaptation, as individuals learn to navigate the unpredictable nature of life with courage and flexibility.

The importance of certainty lies in its ability to provide stability, confidence, and direction in various aspects of life. Here are some key reasons why certainty is important:

1. Clarity and Focus: Certainty provides clarity and focus by eliminating doubt and ambiguity. It helps individuals and organizations understand what they want to achieve and how to get there, guiding decision-making and action.

2. Confidence and Assurance: Certainty breeds confidence and assurance, enabling individuals to approach challenges and opportunities with a sense of conviction and optimism. It instills trust in one's abilities, decisions, and beliefs, leading to greater resilience and perseverance in the face of adversity.

3. Effective Decision-Making: Certainty facilitates effective decision-making by reducing uncertainty and indecision. When individuals have a clear understanding of their goals, values, and priorities, they can make informed choices that align with their objectives and preferences.

4. Risk Management: Certainty plays a crucial role in risk management by allowing individuals and organizations to assess and mitigate potential risks more effectively. With a clear understanding of the potential outcomes and probabilities, they can take proactive measures to minimize negative impacts and capitalize on opportunities.

5. Emotional Well-being: Certainty contributes to emotional well-being by reducing stress, anxiety, and uncertainty about the future. When individuals feel confident and assured about their circumstances and prospects, they experience greater peace of mind and overall satisfaction with their lives.

6. Relationship Building: Certainty fosters trust and reliability in relationships, whether personal, professional, or social. When individuals can depend on each other's words and actions with confidence, it strengthens bonds and facilitates effective communication and collaboration.

7. Goal Achievement: Certainty is essential for achieving goals and objectives, as it provides the clarity and determination needed to stay focused and motivated. When individuals are certain about what they want to accomplish, they can overcome obstacles and persist in their efforts until they succeed.

8. Innovation and Creativity: While certainty is often associated with stability and predictability, it can also provide a foundation for innovation and creativity. When individuals have a clear understanding of the current state of affairs, they can explore new ideas and possibilities with confidence,

knowing that they are building on solid ground.

9. Personal Growth: Certainty facilitates personal growth and development by empowering individuals to take ownership of their lives and pursue their aspirations with conviction. When individuals have a clear sense of direction and purpose, they are more likely to engage in self-improvement activities and seek out new opportunities for learning and growth.

10. Resilience and Adaptability: Finally, certainty contributes to resilience and adaptability by providing a sense of stability and security in times of change or uncertainty. When individuals have a strong foundation of certainty in their beliefs, values, and abilities, they are better equipped to navigate challenges and embrace new opportunities for growth and development.

Certainty is important because it provides clarity, confidence, and direction, enabling individuals and organizations to make informed decisions, manage risks, build relationships, achieve goals, and thrive in an ever-changing world.

The benefits of certainty are numerous and can positively impact various aspects of life. Here are some key advantages:

1. Confidence: Certainty boosts self-confidence, allowing individuals to approach tasks, challenges, and opportunities with assurance in their abilities and decisions.

2. Clarity: Certainty provides clarity of purpose and direction, helping individuals understand what they want to achieve and how to navigate their path forward.

3. Decision-Making: Certainty facilitates decision-making by reducing doubt and ambiguity, enabling individuals to make choices with conviction and confidence.

4. Focus: Certainty helps individuals stay focused on their goals and priorities, minimizing distractions and allowing them to channel their energy and efforts more effectively.

5. Resilience: Certainty strengthens resilience, enabling individuals to bounce back from setbacks and challenges with confidence and determination.

6. Motivation: Certainty fuels motivation, inspiring individuals to pursue their goals and aspirations with enthusiasm and persistence.

7. Emotional Well-being: Certainty contributes to emotional well-being by reducing stress, anxiety, and uncertainty about the future, leading to

greater peace of mind and contentment.

8. Productivity: Certainty enhances productivity by providing a clear sense of direction and purpose, allowing individuals to focus their time and resources on activities that align with their goals.

9. Effective Communication: Certainty improves communication by enabling individuals to express themselves confidently and assertively, fostering understanding and collaboration with others.

10. Success: Ultimately, certainty increases the likelihood of success in achieving goals and aspirations, as individuals are better equipped to overcome obstacles, seize opportunities, and realize their full potential.

Overall, the benefits of certainty extend to various domains of life, including personal growth, professional success, and overall well-being, empowering individuals to lead fulfilling and purposeful lives.

While certainty offers many advantages, it can also have some disadvantages in certain situations. Here are a few potential drawbacks:

1. Closed-Mindedness: Certainty can lead to closed-mindedness, where individuals become resistant to considering alternative perspectives or viewpoints that challenge their beliefs or assumptions.

2. Rigidity: Certainty may result in rigidity in thinking and behavior, as individuals may be unwilling to adapt or change their approach, even in the face of new information or evidence.

3. Overconfidence: Certainty can breed overconfidence, leading individuals to underestimate risks or overlook potential pitfalls, which may result in poor decision-making or judgment.

4. Failure to Innovate: Certainty may stifle innovation and creativity, as individuals may be less inclined to explore new ideas or approaches when they are certain that their current methods are effective.

5. Dismissal of Feedback: Certainty may lead individuals to dismiss constructive feedback or criticism, as they may believe that they already have all the answers and do not need input from others.

6. Resistance to Change: Certainty can make individuals resistant to change, as they may be comfortable with the status quo and reluctant to embrace new opportunities or challenges.

7. Blind Spots: Certainty may create blind spots, where individuals fail to recognize or acknowledge their own limitations, biases, or shortcomings, which can hinder personal or professional growth.

8. Conflict: Certainty can lead to conflict in interpersonal relationships or group dynamics, as individuals may be unwilling to compromise or

consider alternative viewpoints, leading to tension or disagreement.

9. Loss of Opportunities: Certainty may cause individuals to overlook potential opportunities or possibilities, as they may be focused solely on their existing beliefs or goals.

10. Missed Learning Opportunities: Certainty may prevent individuals from being open to learning and growth, as they may believe that they already know everything they need to know about a particular subject or situation.

While certainty can provide a sense of confidence and direction, it is essential to balance it with humility, openness, and a willingness to adapt and learn from new experiences and perspectives.

Improving certainty involves cultivating confidence, clarity, and assurance in various aspects of life. Here are some strategies to enhance certainty:

1. Seek Knowledge and Information: Increase your understanding of relevant topics or areas by seeking knowledge and information through research, study, and exploration. The more you know about a subject, the more confident and certain you will feel about it.

2. Clarify Your Goals and Values: Take time to clarify your goals, values, and priorities in life. Reflect on what matters most to you and what you want to achieve. Having a clear sense of purpose and direction can increase your certainty about your decisions and actions.

3. Set Achievable Milestones: Break down your goals into smaller, achievable milestones or tasks. Setting clear, measurable objectives can provide a sense of progress and accomplishment, boosting your confidence and certainty along the way.

4. Challenge Negative Thoughts: Challenge self-doubt and negative thoughts that undermine your confidence and certainty. Practice reframing negative beliefs into more positive and empowering affirmations that reinforce your abilities and potential.

5. Embrace Failure as Learning: Shift your perspective on failure as an opportunity for learning and growth rather than a reflection of your abilities or worth. Embrace challenges and setbacks as valuable experiences that can strengthen your resilience and increase your certainty in your ability to overcome obstacles.

6. Practice Visualization and Affirmations: Use visualization techniques and positive affirmations to reinforce your confidence and certainty. Visualize yourself succeeding in your endeavors and repeat affirmations

that affirm your capabilities and worthiness.

7. Build Competence and Skills: Invest in building your competence and skills in areas relevant to your goals and aspirations. Acquiring new knowledge or mastering new skills can increase your confidence and certainty in your ability to achieve success.

8. Surround Yourself with Supportive People: Surround yourself with supportive individuals who believe in you and encourage your growth and development. Seek out mentors, coaches, or peers who can provide guidance, feedback, and encouragement as you pursue your goals.

9. Take Action: Take proactive steps towards your goals, even if you feel uncertain or afraid. Action breeds confidence and clarity, as you gain firsthand experience and feedback that can inform your decisions and increase your certainty.

10. Practice Self-Compassion: Be kind to yourself and practice self-compassion as you navigate challenges and setbacks. Treat yourself with the same understanding and empathy that you would offer to a friend facing similar circumstances, and remember that uncertainty is a natural part of growth and exploration.

By incorporating these strategies into your daily life, you can gradually increase your confidence, clarity, and certainty, empowering yourself to pursue your goals and aspirations with greater conviction and assurance.

Examples of certainty can be found in various aspects of life, where individuals or situations exhibit a high level of confidence, assurance, or predictability. Here are some examples:

1. Scientific Laws: Scientific laws, such as the law of gravity or Newton's laws of motion, are considered certain because they describe consistent patterns observed in nature that hold true under specific conditions.

2. Mathematical Principles: Mathematical principles, such as the Pythagorean theorem or the laws of probability, are considered certain because they are based on logical proofs and apply universally across all contexts.

3. Physical Constants: Physical constants, such as the speed of light in a vacuum or the charge of an electron, are considered certain because they have been measured with high precision and remain constant under all known conditions.

4. Legal Precedents: Legal precedents, established through court rulings or legislative acts, provide certainty in the interpretation and application of laws within a legal system, guiding future decisions and actions.

5. Historical Facts: Historical facts, such as dates of significant events or the outcomes of past conflicts, are considered certain based on documented evidence and scholarly consensus among historians.

6. Personal Convictions: Personal convictions, such as deeply held beliefs or values, can provide individuals with a sense of certainty about their identity, purpose, or moral principles, guiding their choices and actions.

7. Expert Opinions: Expert opinions, based on extensive knowledge and experience in a particular field, can provide certainty in decision-making and problem-solving, especially when supported by empirical evidence or consensus among peers.

8. Technical Specifications: Technical specifications, such as engineering standards or software requirements, provide certainty in the design and implementation of products and systems, ensuring reliability and interoperability.

9. Financial Contracts: Financial contracts, such as insurance policies or loan agreements, provide certainty in the terms and conditions governing transactions, reducing risk and facilitating trust between parties.

10. Natural Phenomena: Certain natural phenomena, such as the predictable cycles of the seasons or the orbits of celestial bodies, provide certainty in our understanding of the physical world and our ability to forecast future events.

These examples illustrate how certainty manifests in different contexts, providing stability, predictability, and confidence in our understanding of the world and our ability to navigate it effectively.

When Beyoncé announces a new album release date, fans can be certain that it will drop on that day. Beyoncé has a track record of consistently delivering on her promises, and her team ensures meticulous planning and execution of album releases. Therefore, when Beyoncé announces a release date, fans can trust in the certainty of the album dropping as scheduled, creating excitement and anticipation among her fan base.

When Oprah Winfrey announces a new book club selection, it significantly impacts the literary world. Oprah's book club has a long-standing reputation for promoting meaningful and impactful reads, often resulting in a significant boost in sales and recognition for the selected authors. The Oprah Book Club seal of approval holds considerable significance for both established and emerging writers, as it can lead to increased visibility, book sales, and critical acclaim. Additionally, Oprah's influence extends beyond the literary sphere, as her recommendations often spark conversations and inspire readers worldwide, highlighting the significance of her cultural impact and authority as a tastemaker.

THIRTEEN
FORGIVENESS

Forgiveness is the act of letting go of feelings of resentment, anger, or vengeance toward someone who has wronged you. It involves releasing negative emotions and choosing to pardon or absolve the person from their wrongdoing, regardless of whether they have apologized or made amends.

Forgiveness is not about condoning or excusing the behavior of the person who harmed you, nor is it about forgetting what happened. Instead, it is a conscious decision to free yourself from the emotional burden of holding onto grudges or seeking revenge. It allows you to move forward with your life, heal from the pain caused by the offense, and restore peace within yourself.

Forgiveness is a deeply personal and transformative process that can lead to emotional healing, reconciliation, and growth. It requires empathy, compassion, and a willingness to cultivate understanding and empathy for both yourself and the person who hurt you.

Forgiveness is an act of self-care and empowerment. By choosing to forgive, you reclaim your power and refuse to let past hurts define your present and future. It allows you to break free from the cycle of resentment and bitterness, opening the door to greater emotional well-being, inner peace, and personal fulfillment.

Forgiveness is a crucial aspect of personal life that can profoundly impact emotional well-being, relationships, and overall quality of life. Here are some key reasons why forgiveness is important:

Emotional Well-being

Reduces Stress and Anger: Holding onto grudges and resentment can cause chronic stress and anger. Forgiveness allows you to let go of negative emotions, reducing overall stress levels.

Improves Mental Health: Forgiving others can alleviate symptoms of anxiety and depression, leading to improved mental health and a more positive outlook on life.

Promotes Inner Peace: Forgiveness can bring a sense of inner peace and emotional freedom, allowing you to move forward without the burden of past grievances.

Physical Health

Lowers Blood Pressure: Letting go of anger and resentment can lead to lower blood pressure and reduced risk of heart-related issues.

Enhances Immune Function: Chronic stress from holding grudges can weaken the immune system. Forgiveness helps reduce stress and supports a healthier immune response.

Improves Sleep: Forgiving others can lead to better sleep quality by reducing stress and anxiety, which often interfere with restful sleep.

Relationships

Strengthens Bonds: Forgiveness is essential for healing and maintaining healthy relationships. It fosters trust, understanding, and emotional closeness.

Encourages Empathy and Compassion: Forgiving others encourages empathy and compassion, allowing you to see situations from different perspectives and promoting deeper connections.

Reduces Conflict: Forgiveness helps resolve conflicts and prevents them from escalating, contributing to more harmonious and stable relationships.

Personal Growth

Promotes Self-Reflection: The process of forgiveness often involves self-reflection and understanding your own feelings and motivations, which can lead to personal growth and self-awareness.

Encourages Letting Go: Learning to forgive helps you let go of past hurts and focus on the present and future, fostering a more positive and proactive mindset.

Builds Resilience: Forgiveness can build emotional resilience, helping you cope with future challenges and conflicts more effectively.

Spiritual and Moral Development

Aligns with Moral and Ethical Values: Many spiritual and moral teachings emphasize the importance of forgiveness. Practicing forgiveness can align your actions with these values, fostering a sense of integrity and purpose.

Fosters Humility: Forgiveness involves acknowledging that everyone makes mistakes, including yourself. This fosters humility and a more balanced view of yourself and others.

Promotes Compassionate Living: Forgiving others encourages a compassionate and kind approach to life, benefiting both yourself and those around you.

Forgiveness offers numerous benefits for both your mental and emotional well-being. Here are some of the key advantages of practicing forgiveness:

1. Reduced Stress: Letting go of resentment and anger through forgiveness can lower your stress levels and promote relaxation. By releasing negative emotions, you can experience greater calmness and peace of mind.

2. Improved Mental Health: Forgiveness is associated with improved mental health outcomes, including reduced symptoms of depression, anxiety, and trauma-related stress. It can help you break free from rumination and negative thought patterns, leading to greater psychological resilience.

3. Enhanced Physical Health: Forgiveness has been linked to improved physical health outcomes, such as lower blood pressure, reduced risk of cardiovascular disease, and enhanced immune function. By reducing stress and promoting emotional well-being, forgiveness can contribute to overall physical health.

4. Better Relationships: Forgiveness fosters healthier and more satisfying relationships by promoting trust, empathy, and understanding. It allows you to let go of grudges and resentments, paving the way for reconciliation, communication, and intimacy.

5. Increased Self-Esteem: Forgiving yourself and others can boost your self-esteem and self-worth. It allows you to recognize your own capacity for growth, resilience, and compassion, leading to greater self-acceptance and confidence.

6. Greater Resilience: Forgiveness builds resilience by helping you bounce back from adversity and overcome challenges more effectively. It encourages adaptive coping strategies and a positive outlook on life, even in the face of setbacks or disappointments.

7. Spiritual Growth: Forgiveness is often a core principle in many spiritual and religious traditions. It fosters spiritual growth by promoting virtues such as compassion, humility, and acceptance, and by deepening

your connection to others and to a higher power.

8. Liberation from the Past: Forgiveness allows you to break free from the chains of the past and embrace the present moment with greater freedom and openness. It empowers you to release old wounds and move forward with renewed purpose and clarity.

9. Promotion of Social Harmony: Forgiveness contributes to social harmony by fostering reconciliation, understanding, and cooperation within communities and societies. It promotes empathy and compassion, laying the foundation for peace and reconciliation.

10. Personal Growth and Transformation: Forgiveness is a transformative process that can lead to personal growth, wisdom, and insight. It challenges you to confront difficult emotions and experiences, leading to greater self-awareness, empathy, and resilience.

Forgiveness offers a multitude of benefits that can enhance your quality of life, strengthen your relationships, and promote overall well-being. By practicing forgiveness, you can experience greater peace, joy, and fulfillment in your life.

While forgiveness is generally associated with numerous benefits, there are also potential disadvantages or challenges to consider:

1. Perceived Weakness: Some individuals may perceive forgiveness as a sign of weakness or vulnerability, especially in cultures or contexts where forgiveness is not valued or encouraged. This perception can lead to reluctance or resistance to forgive.

2. Risk of Repeated Harm: Forgiving someone who has repeatedly hurt or betrayed you may increase the risk of future harm if the person continues to engage in harmful behavior without consequences. Forgiveness does not necessarily mean reconciliation or trust restoration.

3. Emotional Vulnerability: Opening yourself up to forgiveness can make you emotionally vulnerable, particularly if you have been deeply hurt or betrayed. There is a risk of experiencing further pain or disappointment if the forgiven individual fails to acknowledge or appreciate your forgiveness.

4. Misinterpretation of Forgiveness: Offering forgiveness may be misinterpreted as condoning or excusing the behavior of the person who wronged you, especially if they do not fully understand or acknowledge the impact of their actions. This can lead to misunderstandings or further conflict.

5. Delayed Healing: In some cases, forgiveness may be premature or incomplete, leading to delayed healing or unresolved emotional wounds.

Rushing the forgiveness process without fully addressing underlying emotions or grievances can hinder true reconciliation and healing.

6. Internal Conflict: Struggling with feelings of resentment or anger after forgiving someone can create internal conflict and distress. You may experience guilt or self-doubt for not being able to fully let go of negative emotions, despite your efforts to forgive.

7. Sense of Injustice: Forgiving someone who has wronged you may feel unjust or unfair, especially if the person has not faced consequences for their actions. This can lead to feelings of resentment or bitterness toward the perceived lack of accountability.

8. Rebuilding Trust: Forgiveness does not automatically restore trust in relationships. Rebuilding trust requires consistent effort, honesty, and accountability from both parties, which can be challenging and time-consuming.

9. Unresolved Trauma: Forgiveness may not address underlying trauma or emotional wounds caused by the wrongdoing. In some cases, professional counseling or therapy may be necessary to process and heal from the trauma, even after forgiveness has been offered.

10. Boundary Setting: Forgiving someone does not negate the need for healthy boundaries in relationships. It's important to establish and enforce boundaries to protect yourself from further harm, even after forgiveness has been extended.

It's essential to consider these potential disadvantages and challenges when navigating the forgiveness process. Forgiveness is a complex and deeply personal journey that may require time, introspection, and support from others.

Improving forgiveness is a gradual process that requires self-reflection, compassion, and a willingness to let go of resentment. Here are some steps you can take to cultivate forgiveness:

1. Practice Self-Compassion: Recognize that forgiveness is as much about releasing yourself from pain as it is about absolving the other person. Be kind to yourself and acknowledge the difficulty of the situation you're facing.

2. Understand the Benefits of Forgiveness: Educate yourself about the positive impact forgiveness can have on your mental and emotional well-being. Understand that forgiving doesn't mean forgetting, but rather freeing yourself from the burden of resentment.

3. Cultivate Empathy: Try to understand the perspective of the person who wronged you. Consider what may have led them to behave in hurtful ways and recognize that everyone makes mistakes.

4. Reflect on Your Feelings: Take time to reflect on the emotions you're experiencing, such as anger, sadness, or betrayal. Allow yourself to feel these emotions without judgment and explore their underlying causes.

5. Practice Mindfulness: Incorporate mindfulness practices into your daily routine, such as meditation or deep breathing exercises. These techniques can help you stay present in the moment and reduce the intensity of negative emotions.

6. Set Boundaries: Establish healthy boundaries with the person who hurt you to protect yourself from further harm. Communicate your needs clearly and assertively while maintaining compassion and understanding.

7. Seek Support: Reach out to trusted friends, family members, or a therapist for support and guidance as you navigate the forgiveness process. Talking about your feelings with others can provide validation and perspective.

8. Let Go of Resentment: Gradually release feelings of resentment and anger toward the person who wronged you. Remember that forgiveness is a choice and a process, and it may take time to fully let go of negative emotions.

9. Focus on Healing: Engage in activities that promote healing and self-care, such as journaling, spending time in nature, or pursuing hobbies you enjoy. Prioritize your well-being as you work toward forgiveness.

10. Practice Forgiveness Daily: Incorporate forgiveness into your daily life by extending compassion and understanding to yourself and others. Practice forgiveness not only for past grievances but also for everyday frustrations and conflicts.

By integrating these strategies into your life, you can gradually improve your ability to forgive and experience greater peace, resilience, and emotional well-being. Remember that forgiveness is a journey, and be patient and compassionate with yourself as you work toward healing and reconciliation.

Here are a few powerful examples of forgiveness that demonstrate the transformative nature of this act:

1. Nelson Mandela: After spending 27 years in prison for his anti-apartheid activism, Nelson Mandela famously forgave his captors and worked towards reconciliation in South Africa. Instead of seeking revenge

or harboring resentment, Mandela embraced forgiveness as a cornerstone of the country's transition to democracy, promoting healing and unity among its diverse population.

2. Eva Mozes Kor: A Holocaust survivor, Eva Mozes Kor forgave the Nazis and the perpetrators of horrific experiments conducted at Auschwitz, including Dr. Josef Mengele. Despite enduring unimaginable suffering and loss, Kor chose to forgive as a way to free herself from the burden of hatred and reclaim her own humanity. She dedicated her life to promoting forgiveness and reconciliation through her work as a speaker and educator.

3. Pope John Paul II and Mehmet Ali Ağca: In 1981, Mehmet Ali Ağca attempted to assassinate Pope John Paul II in St. Peter's Square. Despite being shot and gravely wounded, the Pope publicly forgave Ağca and even visited him in prison to offer his forgiveness in person. This act of forgiveness shocked the world and exemplified the Pope's commitment to the principles of compassion and reconciliation.

4. The Amish Community of Nickel Mines: In 2006, a gunman entered an Amish schoolhouse in Nickel Mines, Pennsylvania, and killed five schoolgirls before taking his own life. In the aftermath of the tragedy, members of the Amish community shocked the world by extending forgiveness to the gunman's family and offering support and compassion to his widow and children. Their act of forgiveness and reconciliation demonstrated the power of grace and compassion in the face of unimaginable loss.

5. Desmond Tutu: As the Chair of South Africa's Truth and Reconciliation Commission, Desmond Tutu played a key role in promoting forgiveness and reconciliation in the aftermath of apartheid. Through the commission's work, Tutu encouraged both victims and perpetrators to come forward, share their stories, and seek forgiveness as a path towards healing and national unity.

These examples illustrate the profound impact of forgiveness in promoting healing, reconciliation, and peace in the face of adversity and injustice. They remind us that forgiveness is not a sign of weakness, but rather a courageous and transformative act that can break the cycle of violence and hatred, and inspire hope for a better future.

One notable example of forgiveness demonstrated by a celebrity is the story of Beyoncé Knowles and her father, Mathew Knowles.

Mathew Knowles served as Beyoncé's manager for many years, overseeing her rise to fame as a member of Destiny's Child and later as a solo artist. However, their professional relationship became strained, and in 2011, Beyoncé announced that she was parting ways with her father as her manager.

Despite the challenges in their relationship, Beyoncé has publicly expressed forgiveness and understanding towards her father. In interviews and through her music, she has spoken about the complexities of their dynamic and the importance of forgiveness in moving forward.

In her visual album "Lemonade," Beyoncé explores themes of betrayal, forgiveness, and redemption, including her relationship with her father. Through powerful lyrics and imagery, she reflects on the pain caused by his actions but ultimately chooses to forgive him and reconcile their relationship.

This example highlights the transformative power of forgiveness, even in the context of complex family dynamics and professional relationships. Beyoncé's willingness to forgive her father demonstrates maturity, compassion, and a commitment to healing and reconciliation, inspiring others to embrace forgiveness in their own lives.

Lord Mahavir, the 24th Tirthankara of Jainism, is known for his teachings of non-violence (ahimsa), compassion, and forgiveness. His life and teachings serve as an inspiration for millions of people around the world.

Throughout his life, Lord Mahavir demonstrated forgiveness towards those who wronged him, teaching his followers to cultivate compassion and forgiveness in their own lives. His teachings emphasize the importance of letting go of anger, resentment, and hatred, and embracing love, compassion, and forgiveness as essential virtues on the path to spiritual liberation.

The story of Lord Mahavir's forgiveness serves as a timeless reminder of the power of forgiveness to heal wounds, transform lives, and foster peace and harmony in the world. It inspires individuals to cultivate forgiveness in their own hearts and extend compassion and understanding to all beings, regardless of past actions or differences.

About The Author

Krunal Shah holds a Master's degree in Information Systems from the USA and has nine years of experience working for various companies across the United States. He relocated to India to pursue his passions and has since diversified into multiple entrepreneurial ventures over the past decade. Krunal Shah is the founder of a gold jewellery business, a mental health coaching business, and a digital marketing business, reflecting his expertise in commerce and personal development fields.

Contact Information:
Email: Sambhavkrunalshah@gmail.com
Instagram: Krunalshah09
YouTube: Krunalshah09